The Grand Tour Files 2020

Pro cycling tales from a social distance

By Pete Linsley

(www.road-theory.com)

For Katy, Joe, and Jim

Contents

Super-Spreading

Imagine you were tasked with designing an event to propagate a virus further and wider across a continent. First of all, you might question the motives of your employer. But should you accept the challenge, your event might well look like a Grand Tour. A thousand-strong caravan of riders, staff, journalists, liggers, and hangers-on moving from town to town, in and out of every hotel from Sicily, via Nice and Paris, to Madrid. A spectacle to which people traditionally gather at the roadside, get as close as possible to each other, and bellow with open-mouthed saliva spraying excitement.

On one hand we have a public health emergency. On the other, several dozen skinny blokes racing bikes to win a colourful t-shirt. Let's agree that pro cycling is the least important of those two things, and that staging a bike race in 2020 was something of a balancing act. Especially when that bike race was a three-week long Grand Tour and you have every intention of doing it three times in three countries.

Eek.

Covid-secure 'bubbles' were formed. Team-branded masks were de-rigeur. And while France and Italy, to some degree, saw fans (at least thinly) lining the roadside, by the time we reached the Vuelta Espana Covid enforcement was in full effect. To see the riders scaling atmospheric mountain peaks, the usual claustrophobic phalanx of fans reduced to a smattering of race officials, team helpers, and the occasional lonely police officer, was a little dispiriting. But back in April and May, the idea of *any* of these races taking place was a long shot. So when the racing finally began we trusted that it was all nice and safe and gladly lapped up what was on offer.

We had a late August Tour de France that led into an autumnal and weather-beaten Giro d'Italia. That the Giro could be moved, just like that, from its traditional May slot, further proof that during a pandemic everything seems possible. In this most conservative sport a simple calendar re-jig is basically a revolution. As if to compound the chaos, the Vuelta Espana would begin with the Giro still ongoing – overlapping Grand Tours, no less! – and would rumble on in slightly wintery fashion into November.

Propose any of this back in 2019 and you'd have been met with a: 'Pffsshh! Non. C'est ridicule.' Waved away to have a good long think about the lunacy of your ideas. But against the odds we found ourselves treated to three exciting, surprising, occasionally weird and unsettling, but highly entertaining Grand Tours.

Three positives, for want of a better adjective, in a terrible year.

Authors note: when I name riders during this book, I will add their team name in brackets, the first time they appear in each Grand Tour. From there I will avoid continuing to name them for reasons of neatness, and to keep out of your way.

Tour de France

Pre-Tour we can say this much: the race will begin on Saturday 29th August 2020. It will then unfurl itself seductively, and with increasing jeopardy, across the chaise longue of France.

The hastily cobbled together rules dictate that two positive Covid tests in a single team mean the race is over for them. It's not hard to imagine a whole *rash* of positives. How on earth do you prevent that, packed together in a peloton out on the road? The race could get very thin indeed.

Normally we'd be making predictions about Bernal and Roglic, Dumoulin and Pinot, maybe the odd Alaphillippe here and the occasional Miguel Angel Lopez there. We'd be salivating and lip smacking at the prospect of the riders climbing the Grand Colombier and the Col de la Madeleine, and time-trialling up the atmospheric Planche des Belle Filles. At home on our sofa, cushions plumped, a fluffy Credit Lyonnaise Lion mascot to hand and a range of drinks and snacks within our wingspan, we are TOUR-READY!

But we don't really know what to think. We're not sure if this whole bike-racing-through-a-pandemic is a good idea. And we certainly don't know who is on form. We've seen riders doing computer game lockdown racing on Zwift, and we've had a month of harem-scarem catch-up racing on the *actual* roads of *actual* Europe, but we haven't got our usual season-to-date yardsticks. Who will have the hard-won legs to be holding good form in three-weeks-time? Will we even still have a race by then?

We are cautious, trepidatious, conflicted, and ready to be swamped by the utter joy of another Tour de France.

Stages 1-3: Covid Secure on the Côte d'Azur

1: the truce will out

The race, finally, after weeks of delay, is underway. And we have questions. Will it even reach Paris? What about the Alps? The Pyrenees? Or will an outbreak intervene and leave a high ranking French public-health official, technically the winner, resplendent in the Yellow Jersey?

And then, with a mere hundred kilometres complete, another pause. A truce is called. The riders, looking around for an elder statesman to call the shots found German veteran Tony Martin (Team Jumbo-Visma) happy to oblige. Sitting up at the front of the peloton he gave the internationally recognised signal for *'settle down lads, easy does it, this doesn't look safe.'* Upright, like a gently flapping albatross, a bird-like calm descended over the race.

The Stage 1 of our pre-race imagination had us looping around the sunshine city of Nice for a high-stakes day of racing on sun-baked Mediterranean roads. The promise of a Tour de France Yellow Jersey for the winner offering the biggest of all the pro cycling prizes. But Nice (with its fabled two-hundred and sixty days of annual sunshine, lest we forget) let the side down. Of all the days to bucket down with rain it chose day one of this most precarious of Tours de France.

Racing at anything close to full-pelt was not panning out well. With a steady stream of mishap and accident on the sodden roads the penny of caution dropped. Riders, usually at the very pinnacle of cycling mastery, were unable to stay upright. In any other sport a safety-related rule or regulation would kick in, but this is cycling. That would be too obvious. It's left to a senior rider to call the shots. For the safety of all involved Big Tony neutralised proceedings.

Astana Pro Team, always delighted to play the role of pantomime villains, were having none of it. Omar Freile (Astana) ignored the communal caution, hit the front, and slowly cranked up the speed on yet another glassy descent. A couple of teammates took the bait and latched on. I tried, offered Martin, shrugging. Within moments, third wheel Miguel Angel Lopez (Astana) had slipped, skidded across the Tarmac, and face-planted a road sign. Mid-slide, pre-plant, the Colombian may even have found a moment in which to dwell on the concept of comeuppance. This was the very definition.

Sheepish, the Astana rebels soaked back into a pedestrian peloton to shrugs, finger wags, and a general told you so vibe from their colleagues. The moral of the story: listen to Tony.

The peace held for thirty kilometres. The trail of the day's crash victims (more than eighty of them, from a start list of one hundred and seventy-six) eventually reconnecting with the peloton for a final twenty-kilometre drag-race. And we sensed, after a day of such chaos, the finish would not be incident free. The atmosphere still felt lairy. And while we don't want anyone to get hurt, we have shielded, distanced, and locked-down in recent months so that our favourite sport may open up and entertain us. We're not going anywhere without our big finish.

And so, one final crash. Riders strewn across the road, commentators peering for crumpled contenders, and there was Thibaut Pinot (Groupama-FDJ). Catastrophe! Calamité! Everyone's favourite French challenger sprawled and gashed, face like thunder, all emotion and Gallic gesture. Sent a-tumbling in the general hubbub of the race.

Thibaut does not need a fight in the gutter; this is not his natural habitat. To win le Tour he needs stars to align and events to conspire. To see him scattered hither and thither on day one is enough to give Pinot watchers the world over a knot in the stomach. He would pick himself up, and finish in one piece, but this does not bode well.

The sprinters, meanwhile, were away in the distance and hunting that Jersey. Motivated. Caleb Ewan (Lotto-Soudal), Peter Sagan (Bora-Hansgrohe), Sam Bennett (Deceuninck-Quickstep), and Cees Bol (Team Sunweb) punched and counter-punched only for Norwegian heavyweight Alexander Kristoff (Team UAE Emirates), with one huge swing, square on the collective chin of his rivals, to surge clear and win. Boom!

For the amiable thirty-three-year-old a third career Tour Stage win and a Yellow Jersey (size XL) across his massive back. Coronavirus, amid the carnage and chaos, pushed to the back of our minds. At least for a day.

2: three dots and a dash

For Stage 2 Nice got its act together. Whoever is in charge of the big lever marked 'sun' found it, and cranked it, and a stream of pure gold burst forth. The unusual autumnal slot of this Tour de France showed itself in the slight length of the September shadows – not the scorching heat of a July race – but still: dry Tarmac and happy cyclists.

But happiness is relative. To those of us at home, propped on a comfy chair, pampered with the convenience of a quiet life, this looked for all the world like a lovely bike ride in the sun. For the riders it was somewhat tougher. The Maritime Alps, rising from the streets of Nice, are the stuff of pro cycling legend. These fixtures of the traditional early season Paris-Nice stage race are hard and demand to be ridden.

With the descent of the Col de Turini, we were treated to one of those classic, achingly beautiful sequences so beloved of this bike race. The TV helicopter peered down on a tagliatelle of Tarmac draped across the mountainside, the peloton strung out through three or four hairpins, descending on a string, back and forth like a kid's caterpillar toy. The money shot. Coming soon to a highlight reel near you. From the Turini, with the Col d'Eze, the Col de Quatre Chemins, and a town centre finish line in Nice, came the race. Pretty pictures now second fiddle to stone-cold serious game faces.

Front and centre, the yellow menace of Team Jumbo Visma gripped the Col d'Eze like a vice. They flocked at the head of the race and took control. An attempt to whittle down the race, weed out one or two rivals, and generally stamp some very visible authority on proceedings. But Julian Alaphilippe (Deceuninck-Quickstep) is not a man to be intimidated by such behaviour. Unimpressed by qualities such as 'organisation' and 'strategy,' he's a free spirit. And a finish like this – descent, punchy climb, descent – might even have been (literally) designed with our goatee-bearded French pal in mind.

On the Quatre Chemins came an attack from him so telegraphed it might have been launched by the great Samuel Morse himself. With a couple of dots and a dash King Julian was clear. Swiss rider Marc Hirshi (Team Sunweb), a twenty-two-year-old pup, and confident Brit Adam Yates (Mitchelton-Scott), boldly followed. It was immediately clear; our stage winner would come from these three. Norwegian Alexander Kristoff would cede his Yellow Jersey to someone more wiry.

Heading for the finish, Alaphilippe reeled off each of his ticks. He tightened his shoes; adjusted his jersey; casually scratched the back of his head like a Sunday cyclist considering a coffee stop. Each move a casual cue to communicate a general message: I'm so relaxed, this is all very ordinary for me...the Tour de what, you say?

With the line in sight, and the peloton snorting, snarling, and gaining, our buccaneer refused to die wondering. Launching left, Yates was beaten within a pedal stroke. The precocious Hirshi pushed and pulled to within inches but Alaphilippe was uncatchable. The Stage. The Yellow Jersey. A swinging right-hook fist on the line and tears and cuddles to follow.

Back in 2019, Alaphilippe came within a beautifully trimmed whisker of Tour de France glory. We strap ourselves in for another ride.

Yellow Peril

In France, the Yellow Jersey holds a special place. It's venerated. As French journalist Pierre Carrey has it: "it belongs to the Tour leader, and him alone. He's like Louis XIV, the Sun King, reincarnated in a cycling jersey."

And yet Team Jumbo Visma, the Dutch team of race-favourite Primoz Roglic, wear yellow. Every day. With impunity. Sure, it's a kind of dark, off-yellow to the purity of the Yellow Jersey, but it's yellow. The race leader should stand-out – radiant and resplendent - and instead finds himself diluted by eight imposters.

'There he is, the Yellow Jersey, our race leader,' our commentary team inform us, with suitable respect, 'unless it's one of Primoz Roglic's domestiques ferrying drinks and snacks from the team car. Hard to tell from here.'

Surely the Tour bosses should have a word? Lay claim to the ownership of their colour. Embrace the idea of race-leader as Sun King?

Unless you're in Yellow, you can't wear yellow. Simple as that.

3: champagne and canapes

Much of Stage 3, through Provence to Sisteron, was not about Yellow but Polka Dots. The King of the Mountains. One of those early stages where a couple of sprightly contenders leap away up the rood to bag as many minor mountain points as possible.

The aim of the game is to snatch the Jersey and hold it for as many post-stage podium photo opportunities as possible while sponsors schmooze, and backslap, and dine out on the occasion. "OK lads," the team bosses confirm, "today we attack...let's get out there and JUSTIFY that catering budget!"

Our breakaway was entirely French. Benoit Cosnefroy (AG2R La Mondiale) and Anthony Perez (Cofidis) with a plan to crest the climbs up front and hoover up the points. Jerome Cousin (Total Direct Energie), meanwhile, was our guide to the majesty of the Provencal countryside as it wafted by; bearded, mirror-shaded, luxurious pony-tail flowing behind like a brooding bounty hunter on a cheap US TV drama. Clear of his companions, effortlessly dramatic, he sliced through gorges, clung to hillsides, and wended his way between a historic citadel here and an ancient olive grove there. In a world where cyclists are, alas, billboards, this was great screen-time.

Cosnefroy would end the day as mountain leader, in small part due to a relentless pursuit of each summit, and in large part to a crash, by Perez, into his own team car; a broken collarbone, fractured rib, and collapsed lung a more than justified trio of reasons to abandon. Ouch!

Brutal.

Job done for the breakaway, that we would get our sprint finish was never in doubt. Cousin knew he would be reeled in and swallowed up by the peloton, the prospect of a Tour Stage win for a gaggle of adrenaline-fuelled sprinters would see to that, and so with twenty kilometres to go the stage came alive.

Into Sisteron, the sprint would be complicated by two key factors.

First, for a town of such history Sisteron is home to an awful lot of road furniture. Either the Roman settlers in these parts had predicted the twenty-first century challenges of traffic management, or the local infrastructure budget has been diligently maxed out in recent years. Either way, take the wrong side of a roundabout or misjudge a traffic island and it's game over.

Second, obstacles negotiated, came a finishing-straight headwind. Patience and a late surge had to be the tactic du jour. Stay sheltered, wait in the wings, and then pounce!

But this is le Tour, and teams and riders face huge pressure to succeed. A Stage 3 sprint finish is an opportunity to crown a 'successful' Tour as early as the first week. Patience and poise were in short supply, I favour of a desperate, grasping desire to win.

Peter Sagan, on the finishing straight, attacked early. Sam Bennett tracked him and leapt past. Caleb Ewan, meanwhile, paused, and waited, before launching a stunning surge from miles back. Tiny, elfin, forehead against the Tarmac, he ducked beneath the wind, wove past Sagan along the barrier, then veered left like a fly avoiding a swat to dominate the finish. That aerodynamic position of his never looking so timely.

Brave, and bold, it was career Tour Stage win number four. The roar across the line a great valve-release of pressure for Ewan and his Lotto-Soudal team. The Champagne and canapes are being lined up at the team hotel as we speak.

Standings after Stage 3

Yellow Jersey: Julian Alaphilippe

2nd Adam Yates (+4 seconds)

3rd Marc Hirschi (+7 seconds)

Green (sprint/points): Peter Sagan

Polka dots (mountains): Benoit Cosnefroy

Stages 4-5: Power Moves from Jumbo-Visma

4: not so fast, sunshine!

With three stages done the storyline is still not set. We know that Julian Alaphilippe has lost none of his boyish gusto; we think Caleb Ewan might be the fastest in a straight (or even weaving, amongst the bollards and along the barriers) line; we are yet to settle on a pronunciation of Benoit Cosnefroy (Con-fwah? Coz-ne-fwah? Ol' Benny-boy?).

As for the General Classification, the fight for the Yellow Jersey is giving little away. The first wispy strands of a narrative are there but we can't yet knit them together into a Tour branded beanie hat and matching Covid face mask.

Ineos Grenadiers (a swift rebranding for Team Ineos having cast them as off-road 4x4 salesmen this season) have been largely anonymous. Either sluggishly off the pace or carrying out some nefarious to-the-letter race plan hatched by Brailsford and his boffins. Designed to first infiltrate the minds, and then the legs, of rivals Jumbo Visma. Current champ and Team leader Egan Bernal (Ineos Grenadiers) has appeared serene. Geraint

Thomas and Chris Froome, unselected, sit at home draining cans of Stella Artois and chucking the crumpled remains at the TV. Probably. Either that or they are 'training hard,' 'recalibrating objectives,' and 'assessing exciting new goals.' Depends how corporate they're feeling.

Team Jumbo Visma, for their part, have placed themselves front and centre, yellow and black, each time the road has headed upwards. Bar the odd daft tumble (Tom Dumoulin here, George Bennett there) they are military in their attention. Primoz Roglic, on parade, a mirror shine to his boots and a steely salute for the regiment, studiously avoiding mishap.

Thibaut Pinot, to the collective in-breath of the French nation, had a pile up on the sketchy run-in of Stage 1. Key lieutenant David Gaudu (Groupama-FDJ) also came a cropper. Currently in survival mode, fighting to stay with the race, Gaudu's recovery is surely crucial to Thibaut's Tour. Bumped, bruised, and a touch emotional, all appears entirely normal (i.e., a bit wobbly and dramatic) chez Pinot. At some point in the next forty-eight hours the nation must surely exhale

And what of Alaphilippe – King Julian - and his famous gusto?

He's playing it cool: I'm not here to challenge for Yellow, honest guv, I'm just a plucky stage-hunter, happy-go-lucky...oh, look at that Yellow Jersey resplendent across my back, how on earth did that happen?

Today, Stage 4, brought us a ski-station summit finish, eighteen hundred metres of altitude at Orcieres-Merlette, and the promise of answers. Or at the very least some suggestions. Not a full high-altitude test but a softener: seven kilometres at nearly seven percent. A tempo drag to sort genuine wheat from definite chaff. And from the early ramps, from a still large peloton of seventy or eighty riders, the pace began to stiffen. Slowly, surely, faster, and more strung out, the field was whittled like an inviting twig in the hands of a diligent boy scout. Pointy at one end, knobbly in the middle, and getting shorter by the kilometre.

By the finale we were rattling along at pace. Roglic's teammate Sepp Kuss (Team Jumbo-Visma) stern jawed and apparently breathing through his ears, and his Slovenian leader in granite faced control. Alaphilippe, all twitchy and yellow, highly visible. Bernal, Pinot, Yates, Lopez, and Pogacar (Team UAE Emirates) hovered. Having watched his muscular teammates wring the breath from his rivals Roglic was compelled to pounce, only to watch Cofidis' Guillaume Martin, at the very moment when Kuss peeled off, effort done, do just that.

I don't know what "not so fast sunshine" is in Slovenian but Roglic was not having that. He bridged to the Frenchman, bringing the aforementioned cast of contenders with him, and outsprinted the lot of 'em for the win.

BLAM!

POW!

A comic-book Batman punching and swiping a roomful of bad guys. Not a time gain but a psychological one, and a stage win. Ominous. "We're the strongest team, I'm the best rider, and you lot will have to do better than that."

5: Wout-standing

What kind of day was Stage 5?

How might I succinctly capture the flavour of the action?

How about this: with forty-seven kilometres remaining Eurosport's Rob Hatch and colleagues began a lengthy riff on Nougat production. The town of Montelimar was nearby, the "Nougat capital of France" no less. As is the way in France, precise percentages of almonds, pistachios and honey are required to denote a genuine, bona-fide slab of the stuff. Three-thousand tonnes are produced per year. Sean Kelly, in the commentary box, is all but addicted to the stuff. Etc. The ticker, top left, now shows forty kilometres. Seven kilometres of Nougat chat; that kind of day.

A meander from Gap to Privas, criss-crossing the Rhone river, saw the peloton largely intact and in battery-saving mode. The threat of wind – head, tail, cross-tail – towards what promised to be a technical town centre finish loomed over proceedings. Scraps of storyline were all we had.

Like Irish sprinter Sam Bennett, for example, snatching on-the-road points from perennial Green Jersey and living legend Peter Sagan to become the virtual Green Jersey. Was our favourite Slovak about to have that garment unceremoniously ripped from his back? Truth be told, Lord Sagan looks below par. His last race win was way back in summer 2019. As if, maybe, being a world class pro-cyclist is not actually the walk in the park we'd been led to believe. Though for context I will add that he looks below par in the context of Peter Sagan, which resembles most of us living our best life.

Could this really be the year when he loses Green, fair and square, on the road, having won it for seven of the past eight years? A prediction of Sagan in decline feels foolish, even heretical. But whatever the long-term prognosis Stage 4 was the day when Bennett did indeed turn the virtual into literal.

Into Privas, that the entire show didn't end up headlong in the barriers was achievement number one. The way was narrow, twisty, and possessed of an obsessive number of roundabouts and general traffic furniture. Clearly the highways department have indulged in one or two long lunches with their colleagues over in Sisteron. We know the French like the whole peeling-the-onion overhead peloton shot but this was insane. The product, dare I say, of the administrative mind of a nation that finds a mere 27% almond content in a confection intolerable.

For our sprint, it was the six-man precision train of Team Sunweb. Crisp in black and white and committed to delivering Cees Bol to the line, versus an assortment of wheel surfing free-spirited opponents.

Caleb Ewan, Bennett, Sagan and Bryan Coquard (B&B Hotels-Vital Concept) hovered but Wout van Aert (Team Jumbo-Visma), the man-who-can-do-it-all, was too much. He pipped Bol on the line for another considerable notch on his crowded bedpost. Not enough that he's won the one-day classics of Strade Bianche and Milan-San Remo this year he's now, apparently, winning Tour de France bunch sprints too.

Tomorrow, Stage 6, will see Peter Sagan wearing a standard team issue Bora-Hansgrohe jersey in place of his Green Jersey. We think he'll be back in Green soon but we can't say for sure. And that detail alone feels a tiny bit like the first inklings of a new era.

Standings after Stage 5

Yellow Jersey: Adam Yates

2nd Primoz Roglic (+3 seconds)

3rd Tadej Pogacar (+7 seconds)

Green (sprint/points): Sam Bennett

Polka Dots (mountains): Benoit Cosnefroy

The Van Aert of Winning

I would love to express surprise at Wout van Aert winning a Tour de France bunch sprint against a collection of bona-fide bunch-sprinters, but I can't. The ship of surprise has sailed. Van Aert is the-man-who-can-do-it-all.

WVA cut his teeth as a cyclo-cross rider, in the tough Belgian bear-pit of that sport. A triple world champion no less. Check out his Wikipedia page: the section devoted to cyclo-cross results is frankly absurd.

He flirted with road racing before emerging fully in 2018. "Strong bloke, but an hour on the cross bike is very different to five hours on the road," we mused. At Strade Bianche in 2018...not so different after all, we discovered. A tough, gritty, mud spattered third place.

And from there, the trajectory continued upwards. Belgian national TT champion; Tour de France stage wins; points winner (and more stages) at the Criterium du Dauphine; occasionally nipping off to decimate the field at some mud-spattered 'cross event. Only a gruesome and career threatening crash at the 2019 Tour de France could derail him, and even modern medicine was ultimately bent to his will.

In 2020, post-lockdown, he emerged a star. Winning Strade Bianche (with startling strength and control). Victorious at Milan San-Remo, on the line, against Alaphilippe. A close second, this time behind Alaphilippe, at the World Championships. And now, in his role as team domestique, a third career Tour Stage win. And who would bet against more?

Tell me he'll win the Tour one day and I'd shrug, powerless to argue. Not because I think he will, necessarily, but because I daren't say for sure that he won't. He's Wout van Aert, after all. The-man-who-can-do-it-all.

Stages 6-7: South Central

6: mountains of the mind

Stage 5, while our collective head was turned by Wout van Aert, had a postscript. A rule, transgressed, left the race commissaires scratching heads, stroking chins, and dishing out punishment.

Julian Alaphilippe, our Yellow Jersey, had taken a bottle from a roadside team helper within the final twenty kilometres. For safety reasons this is not allowed: by this point the action is often reaching a crescendo and is not a good time to be availing yourself of the catering. Spotted, bang to rights, he was docked twenty seconds and elbowed rudely from the top ten. Adam Yates the surprise recipient of Yellow. The days of favours being dished out to Frenchman apparently gone. Sacre, and indeed, bleu!

For Stage 6, Mont Aigoual watched impassively from the horizon. Big, immovable, oblivious to the human need for rules. A flat roll of a day would lead to the climb of the tough, steep, Col de la Lusette, a brief downhill, a long false flat, and a summit finish on the Aigoual. Our finishing peak, as you may be aware, being famous for two reasons: one, it is the subject of maybe the greatest ever cycling book (The Rider, by Tim Krabbe), and two, it's the third most difficult word to pronounce in the

French language behind yaourt (yoghurt) and écureuil (squirrel).

Mont Eh-gwal? Mont Eye-gool? It's a good job Ben-wah Coz-ne-fwah wasn't prominent on today's stage or we'd have found ourself stranded down a linguistic dead-end negotiating a phonic minefield.

For the first time in this year's Tour, it was a day for the breakaway to take the glory. The main contenders were led largely by Ineos on the climbs. It was a gesture. If not quite in defiance at the current dominance of Jumbo Visma then at least a goofy "hey guys, remember us?"

In the break we had birthday boy Neilson Powless (EF Pro Cycling). A bright-eyed and bushy tailed twenty-four-year-old and, fact fans, the first Native American to compete in the Tour. Possible overexcited by these twin milestones Powless burned his matches quickly on the climb by attacking, then counter attacking his own attack. Essentially lighting one match, popping it (lit) back into the box, and watching with glee as the whole thing went up in a sulphuric blaze. It was fun.

Greg van Avermaet (Team CCC), old Goldie-Bike, was a grim presence. Grinding, by no means a specialist climber, to a sturdy third place. Not unimpressive, but arguably the matching bike and helmet combo of the reigning Olympic champ now losing a little of its lustre. Rather like a struggling businessman retaining the scarlet Ferrari purchased at the peak of his net worth whilst unable to service the running costs. Either that or it is, in fact, solid gold, and is playing havoc with his power-to-weight ratio.

Whatever. He trailed the panting, drooling Jesus Herrada

(Cofidis), who himself remained out of reach of the crisp, clean shaven winner, Alexei Lutsenko (Astana). From the moment the Kazakh had asserted himself on the Lusette, and despite never quite dispatching Herrada, Lutsenko always had it. It was a sinuous, calculated, impressive win.

The summit of Mont Aigoual, meanwhile, disappointed. Through our TV screen it resembled a barren wasteland with some barriers thrown up and a finish line drawn across the road in chalk. A plot of French earth with such cultural standing reduced to a car park. Had "The Rider" emerged from the pen a celebrated French author perhaps they'd have made more of it? At the very least some group of local enthusiasts might have recreated a famous scene from the book in a field for the benefit of the TV helicopters; with tractors, a few bales of hay, and the kids from the local école performing a moving homage.

To mark this literary classic shouldn't have been beyond them. As it was - featureless, and without fanfare - perhaps the Aigoual should've been left to our imagination?

7: Wout a difference a day makes

In contrast to the under-appreciated Aigoual, at the start of Stage 7 the impressive Millau viaduct was lingered over and celebrated. Fawned and feted as a monument to French engineering. And it is impressive. The huge span of this great bridge – traversing the Tarn Valley in Southern France - is a thing a country would want to show off; it says we are big, and shiny, and we get things done. If only Tim Krabbe had managed to shoe-horn a massive infrastructure project into his book he might now be a household name.

Once the viaduct was out of the way the murmurs, as they often do, surfaced on social media. It happens every year. Usually around Stage 7. Suggestions that this edition of the Tour is 'boring', 'predictable', 'lacking excitement'. A couple of ho-hum stages and the negativity sets in. But surely every Grand Tour needs a dose of ho-hum? it's the trough that adds height to the peak of the Pyrenean summit finish or the guerrilla warfare of a late race breakaway. It's context. The natural ebb to the flow of a three-week race.

On the route from Millau to Lavaur, however, the teams seemingly agreed with the internet and resolved to spice things up. On paper it looked like a lumpy, Massif Central kind of a stage. Tough roads, not much in the way of flat, but a probable bunch sprint. Over in the Bora Hansgrohe team bus they were brainstorming.

"Right lads, Twitter says this is all a bit boring...any ideas?" wondered team boss Ralph Denk, stepping out from the on-board team-issue Hansgrohe Raindance premium shower, towel around his waist, water dribbling down the aisle.

"How about we just go balls-out from the flag and kick the shit out of everyone?" offered Daniel Oss, the maverick Italian domestique, with a shrug.

"I like it...if we drop Sam Bennett, Peter can sweep up the bonus points and get the Green Jersey back?" suggested Lukas Postlberger, "what you think Pete?"

"I like," agreed Sagan, with an enigmatic nod.

So they did. The pace was ferocious. The likes of Bennett and Caleb Ewan were shelled out the back like a pair of plump pistachios. Our entertainment was underway.

Over in the Ineos team car they were also concerned about the entertainment levels and so they did what Ineos do: they engaged a crack team of boffins to marginal-gain the fuck out of the weather. By feeding twenty-years-worth of data into a massive Excel spreadsheet they established that when the race turns right upon leaving the town of Castres with thirty-five kilometres to go, a hefty cross-tailwind will splinter the peloton like a dry log at the blade of a well-sharpened axe.

At the crucial moment Michal Kwiatkowski (Ineos Grenadiers) and others gave it full gas. Echelons formed as riders spread across the road in search of shelter behind others, and our bike race had become a bare-knuckle brawl. This is the beauty of a cross-wind, and an echelon. Run out of road while seeking shelter and you find yourself spat back into a second group. Then a third. Mikel Landa Bahrain-McLaren) would lose time, as would Tadej Pogacar and Richie Porte (Trek-Segafredo). And I put it to you that nothing – sprints, mountains, sprints up mountains – is more exciting than an echelon in a bike race.

Team Jumbo Visma, of course, remained in tight control of all their faculties and well clear of any peril. Tight control being their modus operandi in 2020. But to their credit, they had also stepped up to address the perceived entertainment deficit.

At breakfast, team boss Richard Plugge held court amongst the tightly regulated selection of nuts, grains, and non-dairy milks.

"Wout, would you like to win today or should it be someone else?" he asked Van Aert, world number-one and the-man-who-can-do-it-all.

"Yes Richard, I would like to win."

"Ok then, win."

"Right, I will."

And he did.

With Ewan, Bennett, and other pure sprinters several miles back down the road and adrift in the crosswinds, Van Aert had the likes of Sagan, Boasson-Hagen (NTT Pro Cycling) and Coquard to deal with. While Sagan bumped and barged like a bouncing bomb and the others blustered and blew, our man Wout simply pedalled, then pedalled harder as he got near to the finish line. Not exciting because there was jeopardy and doubt – there wasn't - but exciting because oh-my-goodness-he's-flippin'-well-won-again!

From here, the race heads off for two days in the high Pyrenees. Adam Yates still has an accidental Yellow Jersey to defend, we've all got lots to talk about, and Twitter seems happy again.

Standings after Stage 7

Yellow Jersey: Adam Yates

2nd Primoz Roglic (+3 seconds)

3rd Guillaume Martin (+9 seconds)

Green (sprint/points): Peter Sagan

Polka Dots (mountains): Benoit Cosnefroy

Any Porte in a Storm

While Richie Porte was losing time in the crosswinds his wife was busily giving birth to a healthy baby daughter.

Some cycling fans may try and tell you otherwise, the worship of suffering being a recurring theme in this great sport of ours, but I'm led to believe that childbirth is even more difficult than riding echelons. Even had they been Belgium ones.

Over cobblestones.

In the pissing rain.

They couple knew, of course, that the birth would likely clash with the Tour. They had a decision to make. Because this is 2020, and we have thankfully moved on from the idea that a pro sportsman missing a game, or a race, or a particularly lairy trip with the boys to a strip-club, would reveal some kind of undefined 'weakness.'

"Painful" was how Porte described his absence from the big moment (to clarify, the 'big moment' being the birth, not the right-turn in Castres and the subsequent crosswinds).

"Go to the Tour, do your thing," wife Gemma had reportedly insisted, pre-race, vis a vis the date clash, "but if I turn the television on and you're at the back of the peloton I'll be a little bit pissed."

Stages 8-9: The Pyrenees

8: vive la france (et au revoir Thibaut...)

The French, for me, are not so much a nation as a form of entertainment. I should add, before I am removed from their collective Christmas card list, that I love them for it. The moods, the insouciance, the way their character seeps out of every utterance and action is a joy. And today, Stage 8, a big ol' day in the Pyrenees, was very French.

First, we had Nans Peters (AG2R La Mondiale). No threat to the overall race leaders he was clear. Rampaging away in the break, nine minutes ahead of the peloton over the massive Port de Bales, with random Russian climber Ilnur Zakarin (Team CCC) in pursuit.

Tongue waggling, Peters wrestled his Eddy Merckx bike beneath him like a TV naturalist taming a wily croc. Zakarin gaining on the uphill bits only to be scuppered by a total inability to ride downhill fast on the other side. Even the religious trinket swaying from his seat-post failed to help. Or, to put it in classic, tactlessly French fashion, as Peters did post-stage: "I saw he was going down like a goat."

Peters, a big brute of a rider, took the stage win

Back down the road, on the climb to the summit of the huge Col de Peyresourde, Julian Alaphilippe also gave us a characterful insight. As a tense game of who-will-blink-first played out amongst the big boys, last year's near-winner attacked with a flourish.

YES! we yelled.

Allez Julian!

Five seconds later, he cracked. Gone. Slipping backwards down the mountain as the race rode away. Attacking, a final act, knowing he was about to crack. Dishing out several seconds of utter panic and crashing out of overall contention on his own terms. Better to live a day as a lion than a lifetime as a lamb. Okay, five seconds as a lion...but the simile stands.

This left Guillaume Martin as the strongest looking Frenchman in a fiercely whittled group of team leaders. Martin being perhaps the most French of all the French cyclists; a philosophy graduate, author, and potential dark horse for le Tour. An athletic intellectual. The essence of the smouldering French enigma.

Which brings us, alas, to Monsieur heart-on-his-sleeve himself, Thibaut Pinot. Ahh, Thibaut. You break our hearts again with your struggles, your brothers-in-arms back-slapping leave-no-man-behind teammates, and your epic levels of sheer humanity. Losing twenty-five minutes (!) you will not win le Tour. Not this year. Maybe not ever.

We assume the after-effects of that Stage 1 crash have hampered and held him back. Ruined his sleep. Played havoc with his emotions. Surviving, rather than thriving, until that brittle link between mind and body cracked. When Pinot is good, lest we forget, he is exhilarating. But our defining image is once more of a broken man. He gave little detail as to the reasons for this bad day but he didn't really need to. Stage 8 was simply his jours sans.

All of which French fascination fails to even touch on the raw tussle of today's Yellow Jersey battle. On the Peyresourde, we reached that point in every Tour de France where the state of each team leader is laid bare. With many kilometres to the final summit, they were left largely without teammates. Roglic, Pogacar, Yates, Quintana (Arkea-Samsic), Lopez and Landa were exposed and forced to show their hand. They would live or die.

Egan Bernal, the reigning Tour winner, had a teammate in current Giro d'Italia champion Richard Carapaz, but appears in a constant state of damage limitation. Guillaume Martin was the free-spirit, looking sprightly, as if born ready to assume the mantle of Great French Hope™. Yellow Jersey Yates yo-yoed but held firm. Roglic gave nothing away. Not a twitch nor a facial expression. Nothing. Quintana, newly happy-go-lucky, toyed playfully with his rivals.

But to a man they were left in the wake of child-star Tadej Pogacar. The man with a thousand pronunciations and the clear man-crush of TV's David Millar. "Just look at him: smooth, lithe, sexy, he's a beauty," as Millar didn't actually say but certainly intimated. Pogacar, with a blistering move, clawed back half of the minute-and-more he lost in the crosswinds of Stage 7.

We learnt a lot today. Not enough to stick the mortgage on any single rider to win, but enough to know who certainly won't. We have a top ten of Yates, Roglic, Martin, Bardet (AG2R La Mondiale), Bernal, Quintana, Lopez, Uran (EF Pro Cycling), Pogacar and Mas (Movistar

Team), and a mere minute between them. I, personally, am now fully behind Guillaume Martin and his undoubtedly doomed attempt to end the thirty-five-year losing streak of la Republique.

Vive la France!

9: Marc Hirschi, folk-hero

As mountain ranges go the Pyrenees is a cracker, and it has a Tour de France party trick. Here's how it works: place a summit around ten or fifteen kilometres from the finish and then have the riders, exhausted from a long day on the ol' push iron, white knuckle the descent into town and sprint for the finish line.

I vividly recall Norwegian Thor Hushovd doing this on Stage 13 of the 2011 Tour into the town of Lourdes, and my heartrate has only recently stabilised. Once upon a time, as a boy, I dreamt of scoring the winning goal in a cup final at Wembley. Since that day in 2011 I picture myself descending like a stone into Lourdes and sweeping past Jeremy Roy with three kilometres to go for the win.

It's as if, with the Pyrenees, the potential Tour stage routes were mapped out first, and only later, through heavy tectonic activity and diligent town planning, did the mountains and the towns appear to join up the dots. Every settlement in these parts nestles conveniently at the base of a famous mountain. The combination of moisture-laden Pyrenean atmosphere, a twisting turning tumble of Tarmac, and several dozen alpha males with money to win and girls to impress works every time.

Our summit today was the Col de Marie Blanque; seven kilometres of ever steepening Tarmac, peaking at a painful fourteen percent. Our hero was Marc Hirschi. A Swiss rider who, this time last year, most of us were barely aware of. A Marc Hirschi could've been a fancy pair of high-end shoes or a Genevan bank for all I knew, instead of a twenty-two-year-old Swiss pro cyclist with a nice line in ninety-kilometre solo breakaways.

At the base of the Marie Blanque he had four minutes over the chasing group. By the summit he'd lost three of those and had Roglic, Pogacar, Bernal, and Landa in pursuit, with a ragged band of further contenders chasing on. Hirschi, like a bird of prey scenting a kill, descended like a bullet. In control but teetering, at each hairpin, and every precipitous bend, on the verge of total disaster.

Utterly, terrifyingly, compelling.

With one and a half measly kilometres to go he was cruelly tagged. The vice-like control of Roglic and co. was enough to catch our man. Spoilsports. But Hirschi appeared unmoved. OK, fine, he said, I'll win it this way, instead of that other way. At the catch, he latched on to the group and settled in for a tow to the finish line. He shook the lactic from his legs. He tightened his shoes like a fighter checking his gumshield: boss move Hirschi, BOSS move!

Roglic, Pogacar, Bernal and Landa wanted the win and the bonus seconds. Hirschi hid behind them until a hundred metres to go and then dug deep – to who knows where – to unfurl the sprint of a man in sight of a town sign on the way back from the café. From fifth, to first...BOOM!

By now I'm on my knees. Go Hirschi, Go, GO!!

Arrrggh! Alas. Pogacar and Roglic, with energy to burn having not soloed through one of the world's great mountain ranges, swept by, to leave our new Swiss friend in third. Justice not done. The universe fluffing its lines. Well, we're having our folk-hero, win or no win, for implausibly almost achieving the improbable at an age when most of us would've taken rising from bed before midday as massive win.

Marc Hirschi, we look forward to a decade of this.

No pressure.

And at the conclusion of that Pyrenean nail-biter we have Primoz Roglic in Yellow (Adam Yates having shelled time while Hirschi was up the road) with Bernal, Martin, and Bardet thirty-ish seconds down. That Roglic would assume the race lead at some point felt inevitable. Will Jumbo-Visma now stick, twist, or denounce any form of gambling in favour of the cold control of a project manager with an impressive Gantt chart?

The rest day, tomorrow, promises high tension. It's Covid-19 tests all round and potential expulsions for positive teams and riders. It's cross-yer-fingers time.

Standings after Stage 9

Yellow Jersey: Primoz Roglic

2nd Egan Bernal (+21 seconds)

3rd Guillaume Martin (+28 seconds)

Green (sprint/points): Sam Bennett

Polka Dots (mountains): Benoit Cosnefroy

Stages 10-11: Flat Roads and Sprint Finishes

10: ends in tears

Post Stage 10, masked up and microphone in his face, Irishman Sam Bennett gave us a collective bit o' something in the corner of our eye.

"I thought I'd be in floods of tears to be honest...I'm just in shock," he said, having snaffled the first Tour de France stage win of his career by a quarter wheel from Caleb Ewan.

"Well, you've won, I'm telling you you've won" replied our interviewer, before dangling his mic around in the silence and waiting. Page one, paragraph one, of the big book o' sports journalism. Sub-section 3a: emotion.

Bennett welled up. "Come on lad," the interviewer didn't actually say but certainly hinted at with his still lingering mic, "let it all out...remember that time in nursery when little Tommy stole yer milk? What about when Max, your dog, had to go off and live on the farm? There you go, give in to it Sam..."

Feeling flooded his body like a squirt of lube onto a parched bike-chain and escaped from his eyes as a salty liquid. Tears, some might call 'em. And why not. He blubbed a few words, thanking his team, Team Boss Patrick Lefevere, and his wife (in that order...), and gave those of us who are entirely comfortable with the idea of a big ol' man crying in public an extra reason to like him. I like to think that somewhere, in a sweaty commentary box, countryman and hardest-man-in-the-world Sean Kelly was also wailing like a baby in need of a rusk. Reports of this, at time of writing, are unconfirmed. It's possible the monotone drawl of King Kelly barely wavered.

Rewind to the start of the day, and the news that every rider in the race had successfully navigated the rest-day Covid test and was clear to ride was welcomed by all. Not so Tour boss Christian Prudhomme. A resounding, mildly embarrassing, Covid-positive. Proof that excessive corporate schmoozing can, in some cases, lead to the contraction of infectious unpleasantness.

While the organisers flapped around desperately in search of someone else suitably qualified to wave a big flag from the sunroof of a mid-range estate car, the riders were faced with a flatter than flat coastal route. A seaside jaunt between the twin Atlantic tourist traps of Ile d'Oleran and Il de Ré.

As we, the collective of generic European cycling fans, washed our morning cornflakes down with bottomless espresso and scanned the sports news for the pre-stage form we were all, as one, visited by the intimate clang of synchronised realisation: we might get (whisper it...) echelons. Last time we had echelons Richie Porte's wife got so excited she spontaneously gave birth! Whatever this time?

The exposed coast, were the wind to blow, would see our standard sprint stage rent asunder. It could, we knew, all end in tears. Teams, and riders, would take no chances, preferring to fight recklessly and with scant regard for the integrity of their own bodies than lose an inch of that narrow coastal road. Jonathan Vaughters, boss of EF Pro Cycling, had issues: "Incredibly dangerous," he said, clarifying that "It'd be fine if it were 1908 and the guys were all twenty minutes apart." I checked. It's not.

We got crashes, lots of them. The peloton winding up the speed and increasing the tension with each town traversed. The wind blew, the race split, reformed, and then split, like the liquid-metal shape-shifting T-1000 in Terminator 2. It was nervous. Jittery. Atmospheric.

Into Il de Ré, and for those still upright and in the mood for it we got our sprint. Bennett, led out by Deceuninck-Quickstep teammate Michael Morkov (pronounced, absurdly to the Anglo-Saxon ear, Mer-koo), looked for all the world like delivering rival Caleb Ewan from his slipstream, and on a plate (as he arguably did on Stage 3), to slip past for the win. Ewan is truly the master at surfing wheels and popping his head out at the finish line to snaffle the win.

Ewan did a bike-throw for the line. Bennett "forgot to" (in his own words), but had enough in hand to hang on by the width of a pint of Guinness. And from there, as we know, came the tears.

11: mano y mano y mano y mano

Our location for the day was Poitiers, a small city in central France. Medieval place. Massive cathedral. You know the stuff. On a day that had always promised a sprint the minor climb through the city streets was the leg-sapping fly in the ointment of our wide, boulevard finish. In the end you could've thrown a blanket over them. Which, to be clear, I'm not advocating. You should never throw any kind of linen over a cyclist. Bad enough in the amateur ranks but in the Tour de France? With all those moving parts? Forget it!

At three kilometres to go the road rose for one kilometre, at around four percent in gradient, which was rather naughty of it. It had the effect of draining any final joules of energy from the lead-out men and presented us with an every-man-for-himself cards-on-the-table kind of a sprint. Mano y mano y mano y mano.

With three hundred metres to go Wout van Aert launched way to early and put, and please excuse my use of a piece colloquial English last heard in the 1970's, the absolute willies up the lot of 'em. You don't launch a sprint at three hundred metres, we all mused, stroking our chins and basking in our many years of hard earnt wisdom. We take great pleasure in knowing what we're talking about; this is the payoff from endless afternoons of being wise after the event in front of the telly.

But then again, he's Wout, and he can do-it-all. He's selfishly tearing up the rules before our eyes and writing a whole new set. Now we're not so sure. That bastard, he'll probably win, we conclude, rolling our eyes at the extravagant talent of the man. We like him, but this is becoming too easy. If only someone could do something?

Enter Peter 'man-of-the-people' Sagan. He shares our pain. I swear that, in delivering a mild shoulder barge on the finishing straight to knock Wout off his stride, he glanced down the camera lens with a knowing nod (that was for you guys!).

While Sagan was busy scuppering the Dutchman, Sam Bennett and Caleb Ewan had another bike throwing competition to decide a winner. This time Ewan took it. The four, spread across the road, could, as discussed, have had a banket gently laid across them. But we've agreed that this wouldn't be ideal. It was close, let's just say that. Half a wheel, no more. Only for Sagan to suddenly find himself a couple of hundred wheels in arrears, relegated to last for his beefy indiscretion in, ahem...nudging Van Aert off his stride.

Right now, little Caleb Ewan is edging it in the sprinting stakes, with two stages to one each for Bennett and Van Aert. Sagan seems grumpy and needs a win. Today's relegation wouldn't have helped and tomorrow is a horrid stage, which might not cheer him up. Two hundred kilometres, with medium mountains, it could suit a puncheur, a true climber, even a highly motivated sprinter. And it takes the race back through the Massif Central which, due to being neither one thing nor another, neither flat nor mountainous, is somehow the hardest place in the world to race a bike.

After the endless weeks of pandemic lockdown our Tour de France, right now, is doing what it's designed to do. It's filling that aching chasm at the centre of our life. Each day a standalone episode in a highly binge-able box-set. Storylines mingle, intertwine, and cross reference each other. One more, okay one more, we mutter, as a new stage cues itself up on our screens. And with each new day things, one way or another, happen.

Standings after Stage 11

Yellow Jersey: Primoz Roglic

2nd Egan Bernal (+21 seconds)

3rd Guillaume Martin (+28 seconds)

Green (sprint/points): Sam Bennett

Polka Dots (mountains): Benoit Cosnefroy

Stages 12-14: From West to East

12: righting the wrongs of the universe

We've seen Marc Hirschi do this before. We grip our seats and breathe sporadically. Twitching and flinching at every curve. Precipitous drops, off-camber Tarmac, the growl of the camera moto drowning out our nervous yelps.

And Hirschi?

Chilled. In control. Blasé.

We know that (currently injured) Belgian Remco Evenepoel is the new Eddy Merckx, and the shiniest of all the current crop of pro cycling golden boys. Which makes twenty-two-year-old old Hirschi the Swiss Evenepoel. It's getting confusing. Whoever has their hand on the crank arm of this conveyor of absurd young talent can they please just flick it off for a bit. Give us a chance. Give, quite frankly, everyone over the age of twenty-three a chance.

The surprise of the day, perhaps, was that the Yellow Jersey group had a (relatively) easy day. Relatively. In the context of France's Massif Central. This rugged plateau which makes up fifteen percent of the area of France being known as renowned breaker of cyclists. We saw barely a kilometre of flat road, little in the way of respite, not Alpine climbs by any stretch but, as my friends here in the Cold Dark North (Google them) of England might say: "stabby bastard hills!"

A breakaway win of some description was the most likely of several dozen outcomes today and we all picked our favourites. De Gendt (Lotto-Soudal)? Trentin (Team CCC)? Maybe a magic Alaphilippe day?

But let's give the credit where it's due. In support of Hirschi, Team Sunweb delivered a total masterclass. Schooling the peloton like a mid-80's Mr Miyagi, waxing on and off to instigate a break, ensure a numerical advantage, and spring-board their young buck to do, let's be honest, a Marc Hirschi. This is what he does. It's his thing. I suggested yesterday you should expect things to happen. Imagine being twenty-two-years-old and already having a thing!?

With ten kilometres to go and after extinguishing some minor threat from behind, his body language said it all. Ignore those stats on the TV screen – speed, time gap, heart rate - and just look at him. He's faster. Better. The man is a killer. You watch this, learn that his mentor is one Fabian Cancellara – swarthy Swiss legend of the sport - and the mind wanders off down the road and fills in the next decade with classics, stage wins, and who knows what else.

He so nearly won Stage 9. Today was less about a first Grand Tour Stage win and more about righting the wrongs of the universe. Putting the very laws of nature and justice in their place. He beat the entire Tour de France peloton, solo, at an apparent canter. It's time to get our heads around the talent of Marc Hirschi. We're going to be seeing a lot of him.

The Young Ones

2020 will be remembered for many reasons; among them, as the year when a generation of Zwift-trained, internet-educated, fully-formed pro cyclists ruled the world.

Proving that a post Y2K birthday is no impediment to success, and with easy access to all the information needed to ride quickly on a bike, they are untethered to the decades of received wisdom that previously acted as a lengthy apprenticeship into the sport. From womb to WorldTour with barely an eyelid batted.

Pro cycling has long thrived on a mysterious, archaic swirl of the way things are done. By drip-dripping the knowledge, the established stars of the sport could protect their status and ensure a seamless transition at a time of their choosing. The moment it became possible to Google such phrases as 'how to measure my FTP' and 'should I really avoid eating the soft centre of the baguette or is that a load of old nonsense', a new generation was empowered.

Et voila!

They are winning races with assurance, race-craft, and regularity. As if born to do so. An entire generation elbowing their elders out the way and to hell with hierarchy.

Marc Hirschi, Tadej Pogacar, Remco Evenepoel (not racing here, but a stone-cold superstar), Egan Bernal (current Tour de France champion), Pavel Sivakov, Lennard Kamna. That's not to mention the undoubted half-dozen I haven't yet heard of waiting in the wings. And the likes of Van der Poel and Van Aert – genuine superstars - are hardly veterans.

The list is lengthy. It will soon be illustrious.

13: high noon on the Puy Mary

On a hard day in the Massif Central it was a stage for a big breakaway. Negotiations, between those with an eye on a stage win and those seeking overall contention, were long and tortuous. Big names, stars of the sport, wanted in, but Yellow Jersey Roglic and his team had a strict door policy in place. No-one with even a sniff of Yellow would be allowed to escape. That our eventual star-studded group was waved clear, a triumph for high-level diplomacy

Seventeen of them: Julian Alaphilippe, Dan Martin (Israel Start-up Nation), Max Schachmann (Bora-Hansgrohe), Dani Martinez (EF Pro Cycling), Lennard Kamna (Bora-Hansgrohe), Benoit Cosnefroy, Remi Cavagna (Deceuninck-Quickstep), and Warren Barguil (Arkea-Samsic)

among them. Mercenaries and renegades, proven winners of bike races. Sure, Primoz me ol' mate, you don't need to worry about us...

No matter how numerous and well stocked, though, the break still needs thinning out for the finish. You can't have all seventeen surviving for a bunch sprint; that's not how it works. Before hitting the tough slopes of the Puy Mary - the day's final obstacle - calculations would be made, efforts delivered, and cards played, to leave us with Max Schachman followed closely by his teammate and countryman Lennard Kamna and Dani Martinez, the threatening Colombian. A threat which derives partly from extravagant talent, underlined recently via a smash and grab overall win at the pre-Tour Criterium du Dauphine, but also a fresh bandido 'tach and goatee across his previously clean-cut mush.

Were Martinez to wander into a clap-board wild-west town looking like this the streets would clear, saloon-bar piano players would pause, and Ennio Morricone would strike up a suitable sound-track in readiness for bloodshed.

Menacing.

Were the win decided by a panel of judges scoring on body language Schachmann would lose. Deep in effort, the German's natural style brings a deliberate shake of the head with every pedal stroke. No, pedal, no, pedal, please stop, pedal, dear God it hurts, pedal...

But he's a classy bike rider. And it was deep into the Puy Mary before Martinez finally reeled him in; still with Kamna in tow and poised to duke it out for the stage win. Cruel on the rictus-faced German. The final kilometre or two, at a masochistic fourteen percent, gave us a slow-motion and highly painful uphill 'sprint.' Kamna blinked first, giving one final effort, but Martinez's gunslinger visage proved well deserved. He didn't draw a six-shooter and fill him full o' lead but instead chose to edge past in muscular style and take the stage. Honourable.

The remaining fifteen members of our break were scattered in dribs and drabs down the road. Way back in the peloton, and well before the summit, Team Jumbo Visma were up to their usual tricks. They dispatched Team Ineos with disdain on the climb. A contemptuous wave of the hand and a move over pal, we're in charge now. Thoroughly enjoying their current Alpha male status. Richard Carapaz (Ineos Grenadiers), the last of Egan Bernal's domestiques, found himself on the receiving end of a withering is that it? from Tom Dumoulin (Team Jumbo-Visma) at the conclusion of his final big effort in service of his leader. And with that, we knew Roglic would be gaining time, Bernal losing it, and the rest would fight for scraps.

Approaching the finish, Roglic pulled clear with only countryman (and rival) Tadej Pogacar able to follow. Roglic in that stock-still I've-done-ten-thousand-hours-of-core-workouts-and-I'm-not-afraid-to-use-them position he assumes when he's feeling dominant. The pair put enough of a dent in their rivals to assume first and second positions in the race overall. Bernal slips to third.

Martinez, meanwhile, wandered silently out of town. Fed and watered, horse rested, and in search of his next showdown.

14: smells like team spirit

There comes a moment in each Tour de France when we conduct a French cycling post-mortem. It occurs to us that this will not be the year. We reflect on the last French winner, Bernard Hinault, in 1985. We enjoy this fact, for a laugh, and the annual talking point it provides, before some of us get a bit wistful. Because a French winner of this great event would be quite a thing.

Thibaut Pinot bailed out of contention a few days ago. Shipping time, he sank like a lovely, handsome old boat with a perennially leaky hull. He rides on in the race but to no avail. The sylph-like Romain Bardet and smarty-pants philosophy student and part-time bike racer Guillaume Martin continued to put up a fight. After Stage 12 they sat third and four overall. We raised a collective hopeful eyebrow. We began to workshop nicknames, just in case, because a French Tour winner NEEDS a nickname.

And then, with Stage 13 – perhaps we jinxed it – Bardet was gone. Abandoned. A heavy crash and a subsequent hell-for leather chase back on revealed a bash to the head. A mild aneurysm (bleeding to the brain) as it was hilariously/terrifyingly explained post-stage. Name me another sport where a competitor would desperately jump back into the fray with an aneurysm for company. And while you're at it, join me in agreeing that pro-cycling REALLY needs to up its medical game and take concussion seriously.

Less dramatically, equally disappointingly, Guillaume Martin also dropped out of contention. He just found the other guys to be stronger, in characteristically philosophical style.

And with that, another year goes by.

As for Stage 14 it revolved, for a while, around the Green Jersey. Current holder Sam Bennett was attacked relentlessly by usual holder Peter Sagan and his team. It was targeted and brutal over a couple of testing climbs. The Irishman, eventually, cracked. Sagan clawed back a slew of points but Bennet remains in the Jersey. A couple of pro sportsmen, happily (!?) self-harming themselves in front of a live TV audience for the honour of owning a lovely Green t-shirt being just one of the ways, along with Bardet's aneurism, you could explain this fantastic, archaic sport to the uninitiated.

Our finish, after all of that, was in Lyon. French capital of food. A place where any old bit of innard and gristle, tarted up and given a name, becomes a delicacy [insert name of your favourite unimpressive, gristly rider, for obvious joke here...what, I've gotta do all the work?].

My surprise new favourite team, Sunweb, hovering around like chess pieces in the hands of a Grandmaster, played a blinder. Working strategically, several moves ahead, they launched the ever grim faced, resolutely round-shouldered Tiesj Benoot (Lotto-Soudal), early (it's pronounced Teesh, pronunciation fans!), to disrupt thoughts of a simple sprint. They backed this up by having Marc Hirshi chase down counter-attackers from other teams (De Gendt, Alaphilippe, and Sagan), and then flung Soren Kragh Andersen (Team Sunweb) off down the Lyonnaise streets with three kilometres remaining.

It resembled a manic city centre criterium: frenzied, noisy, and pulse-racingly exciting. With choreographed brilliance Andersen was clear and could not be caught. A thrilling, surprising, masterclass. Black and white in technicolour.

Standings after Stage 14

Yellow Jersey: Primoz Roglic

2nd Tadej Pogacar (+44 seconds)

3rd Egan Bernal (+59 seconds)

Green (sprint/points): Sam Bennett

Polka Dots (mountains): Benoit Cosnefroy

Stages 15-18: Alps (and pre-alps)

15: pleasure and pain

The Lacets – 'the laces' – du Grand Colombier are laid out, to and fro, across the great shoulder of the Grand Colombier. A stretch of picture-perfect Tarmac. These delicate strands of asphalt sit thirteen kilometres from the summit, at a point where the road emerges from the forest and the views open out. Perfectly positioned for the camera crew to capture the riders in a picture frame. We are in the Jura Mountains, lesser-known cousin of the Alps, and the Lacets are their chance to catch the eye.

Before that point, the stage had already skirted the Colombier upon two of its four roads (the Montee de la Selle de Fromental and the Col de la Biche), leaving us with a final, painful pull up the seventeen kilometres of the Colombier proper. At the base, the Jumbo Visma team of leader Primoz Roglic was still six strong. Reminiscent of a dominant, Froome-centric 2016 Team Sky. Other teams already reduced largely to leaders. Mentally, that's either train on which you need to hitch a ride or an impossible outnumbering.

The drama came, as those foresighted Juran roadbuilders knew it one day would, with thirteen kilometres to go. The laces. This moment, on the 13th September 2020, 3.45 pm UK time, was their moment. The helicopter pulled back for the money shot, the lead group perched and wound ever higher, great views over their shoulders, a sense of altitude and atmosphere revealed. And with that, at the centre of that absurdly, brutally pretty scene, Egan Bernal cracked. The Ineos leader and reigning Tour champ in crisis. Grey of face, sweat beading along that great romanesque nose, we could see, even as the Juran geography showed us each party-trick in its possession, that he was done. Not just flagging but beaten.

Another milestone greened out on the ever-knowing Jumbo Visma Gantt chart. Action number 34: crush Egan Bernal. Tick.

He'll lose five minutes, poor sod, we thought, even as the backdrop ran its fingers through our hair and seduced us with its come-hither eyes. Pleasure and pain in perfect union. The timing, and the ability of this incredible race to deliver, faultless as ever.

Jumbo, as you might imagine, did not relent. Peeling off one by one to leave super-duper-ultra-mega-domestique Tom Dumoulin – Grand Tour winner turned servant to the cause - to suck the last drops of energy from each rival. Three-hundred metres to go and loveable Aussie Richie Porte attacked, gamely, and with no desire to die wondering. Child-star Tadej Pogacar came around him, Primoz Roglic latched on, and that pair capped proceedings with a high-altitude arm wrestle for the stage win and the bonus seconds.

Pogacar took the win. Twenty-one years old, a mere forty seconds behind our continued Yellow Jersey Primoz Roglic, and leaving us all very nearly impressed enough to forgive him the white shorts (unnecessary!). Our Tour, and its remaining six stages, is reduced to Roglic v Pogacar (with a heart-warming 'will Richie get on the podium?' side-story).

At time of writing, no word on what caused Egan Bernal to ship seven minutes and relinquish the race. Surely illness, or injury? Whatever. Our Juran friends and their Lacets can now sit back, satisfied, a glass of vin jaune to hand...it's over to you, Alps!

16: Lennard Kämna is a cheeky boy

Stage 16 was semi-mountainous. Pre-Alp, not technically the Alps but pretty damn hilly. Stage 17, tomorrow, is a whopper. The main General Classification contenders, therefore, would not be expending any more energy today than absolutely necessary. A day, without question, for a breakaway win.

From the flag everyone wanted in. After an hour a big group eventually, stuck, formed an escape, and rode away up the road, and that was the cue for Primoz Roglic's Jumbo Visma teammates to get busy. Robert Gesink (Team Jumbo-Visma) was spotted plumping the cushions and preparing the sedan chair, Wout van Aert was peeling grapes and popping them into his boss's mouth, while Tom Dumoulin wafted him seductively with a big palm leaf fan. Time to chill and soak up the views. Don't expend a drop of energy, Primoz. Don't even think.

The break, meanwhile, eeked out a lead of fifteen minutes. All the while each rider looked around to figure how they were going to approach the task of beating each other. Problem was, looking around revealed exalted company: Alaphilippe; Carapaz; Trentin; Kämna; Sivakov (Ineos

Grenadiers); Barguil; Roche (Team Sunweb)...there were dozens of them. Another star-studded affair. At the risk of belittling the nuance and considerable effort of the day's racing I am going to reduce it to three key efforts.

On the biggest climb of the day, in the final thirty kilometres, to the wonderfully named Montée de Saint-Nizier-du-Moucherotte, Richard Carapaz was pushing on at pace. Alaphilippe responded, sprightly, with a burst of energy. This was effort number one. It was big, but alas not long. Lasting around four seconds, the lights went out as suddenly as, well...some lights going out. Alaphilippe going from big threat to footnote in the blink of an eye.

Effort number two came from Carapaz. Seeing that King Julian had been deposed he unleashed aggression. Ripping a fresh bottle of drink from a roadside helper he looked for all the world like a man to whom some dude down the road had just uttered an insulting "yer mum" joke and he was off to sort them out. Twenty-five kilometres to go. Fire in his belly. BOSH! Surely our winning move.

Approaching the summit, though, the Ecuadorian peered back to see the grimacing face of Lennard Kämna; the only man able to follow his rampaging assault. But the German was suffering like a Dachshund. Carapaz knew he had him. But he didn't have the benefit of our slo-mo replay. The moment Carapaz looked forward again Kämna's grimacing face reset to the stone-cold glaze of a killer. Oh my God, we realised, delighted, as one...he's done him up like a kipper! It's the old rope-a-dope. We all fell a little bit in love with him. What a cheeky boy!

Carapaz emptied the tank to finish the job only for the not-quite-so-tired-after-all Kämna to launch past him, clear, to never be seen again. He time-trialled the twenty kilometres to the finish imperiously, and underlined his name on our growing list of implausibly baby-faced pro cyclists currently ripping up the sport in 2020. Impressive.

This was a prime example of what makes le Tour such a great watch. Yes, the General Classification is a bit dull right now. Roglic is in control, his team might – might - have the Yellow Jersey all but sewn up, but every day, if you zoom your focus in tight, is a fabulously entertaining bike race with a plot, a twist, and a satisfying resolution.

Stage 17 features two gigantic climbs to altitude; firstly, up and over the Col de la Madeleine, and then to the summit of the Col de la Loze above the ski-resort of Meribel. It's the Queen stage. The race could be won, or lost, and could include anything in between. If you only downed tools and snuck away from work when no-one was looking once during this Tour de France, tomorrow would be the day.

17: mega-tough and double-naughty

Back on Stage 15, and the climb of the Grand Colombier, reigning Tour champ Egan Bernal tumbled down the rankings. A reported double whammy of back and knee injury putting paid to any possibility of contention. This morning, prior to Stage 17, he abandoned. And without casting aspersions on the grit and determination of the Colombian superstar, the prospect of a Col de la Madeleine followed by a Col de la Loze would be enough to tempt anyone in two minds to down tools.

Brutal is the go-to descriptor in the cycling fan lexicon to describe such a stage. But that's not enough. It was mega-tough, double-naughty, and super-savage. One might even go so far as to say downright uncivilised.

The upper slopes of the Col de la Loze were tortuous. Had the chaps at the UN been on the blower, post stage, to Tour boss Christian Prudhomme and his mates, to discuss the finer points of the Universal Declaration of Human Rights in relation to bike racing, I would not have been surprised. Rumour has it that mass waterboarding has been mooted as a more humane way of separating the main contenders come the later stages of the next tightly contested Tour de France.

Think of one of those overly-steep novelty climbs of the Giro d'Italia or Vuelta Espana: Monte Zoncolan, perhaps, or the Alto d'Angliru. The Loze is like that but at high, high altitude. The same leg-breaking qualities but with the added fun of thin, oxygen-free air. I'm not sure I've ever seen bike riders suffer more than they did today.

The pressure today was on Tadej Pogacar; the young Slovenian, forty-two seconds behind the slightly older Slovenian (Primoz Roglic). Because he's running out of stages. Between today, and Saturday's time-trial, he must make his move to win this Tour de France. As if it were that easy.

Maybe you've tried accelerating on your bike at two-thousand-three-hundred metres above sea level? How did that go? At altitude, and with so much tiredness in the legs, it becomes less about who rides clear down the road and more about who can avoid slipping back out of contention. Physiologically, two-thousand metres is the magic number.

Above that, strange things happen.

The summit slopes gave us our first look at this soon to-be-mythical Col. The road here was only opened in 2019 and has barely been raced. We watched on, wide-eyed, to see what the fuss was about. Sweeping Alpine meadows, steep ramps, and cruel downhill swoops where altitude gained was lost, to be gained again. The contours of an old-fashioned wooden roller coaster plonked atop a mountain peak. Scream if you wanna go faster? No chance. Any form of forward motion, fast or otherwise, was acceptable.

In the final few kilometres we were down to four: Miguel Angel Lopez, Sepp Kuss, Roglic and Pogacar. Slightly slow motion, but unbearably tense. Each on the brink, liable to crack at any moment. To see a rider falling to pieces, so close to the summit, and losing a couple of minutes, requiring no leap of imagination whatsoever.

Faces were grey and grim. Riders hunched over handlebars, doubled up in effort. President Emmanuel Macron watched on, from a fancy car, like some kind of besuited high-ranking masochist. If you have any concept whatsoever of how painful riding a bike can be, it was a tough watch.

Lopez, in time, dragged himself clear in a glorious display of pure will. No threat to our two Tour leaders he seized the stage win and clambered, exhausted, onto the overall podium. Roglic, meanwhile, led Pogacar. Fans bayed and bellowed, super-spreading, as if Covid might take a day off for the occasion, while the older Slovenian pipped the younger one to gather a further fifteen seconds. And probably, such was the effort, lop a couple of years off his life span.

Pogacar, today, probably saw an already implausible Tour win slip through his fingers. He will dig deep again in the mountains tomorrow, and will give it everything up to La Planche des Belles Filles on Stage 20, but will surely fall just short. Providing he didn't inhale too much Covid on those upper slopes today, Roglic is beginning to look like a Tour de France winner.

Race Radio

Pogacar puts the 'I' in team

Jumbo Visma have their own version of the Team Sky template; the squad is packed with top riders, who ride in support of a sole objective, and spend an awful lot of time controlling the pace of the race to the liking of their leader.

So, when Roglic feels good they can notch up the speed a click or two. When he's having a bad moment, they ease off. If anyone attacks him, a teammate follows and closes it down. For Roglic this is not the armchair ride that some (occasionally even me) would have you believe, but still, when attempting to win the world's biggest bike race it's the preferred option.

The alternative is some version of Tadej Pogacar's current predicament.

He has some firepower in his team – David de la Cruz and Jan Polanc, for example, are no slouches in the mountains – but they alone cannot shepherd their man through. It's been common during this race that even when Roglic still has the likes of Tom Dumoulin, George Bennett, and the incredible Sepp Kuss by his side, Pogacar is surfing wheels. Teammate-free and self-sufficient.

He's the Michelin starred chef who also peels the spuds, washes the pots, and mops the floor at the end of the night.

That Primoz Roglic has such a strong team makes his potential win in this race less noble, romantic, and exciting. Chris Froome suffered his own version of that PR conundrum. But we're human and we're suckers for a plucky narrative. If Roglic wins it's because of his team, if Pogacar does it's in spite of his.

18: Ineos have a warm feeling in their tummy

We are not used to this new, anonymous, Team Ineos. We're used to seeing them centre stage, in the spotlight, hero of the story and first name on the credits. They never simply turn up in France for a quiet lap of the country. And yet seventeen stages in and not a peep. No stage wins, no heroic manoeuvres, and with the struggles and subsequent departure of Egan Bernal, no contender for the Yellow Jersey. For Stage 18, cast free of the shackles, they went rogue. A one hundred and seventy-five kilometre two-man guerrilla raid through the Alps.

It was a relentless day. Not the two-peak set-piece of yesterday, but the cols of the **Cormet de Roseland**, Côte de la route des Villes, **Col des Saisies, Col des Aravis,** and the **Glières Plateau** added up to a gruelling route. Not big or steep enough to have the Yellow Jersey contenders eyeing up time gains, but a tough, tough day on the bike.

With a hundred kilometres to go, the big breakaway group (initially numbering thirty-plus) had been stripped thoroughly of dead wood to leave five, handsome planks of carefully crafted timber in the clear; Michal Kwiatkowski and Richard Carapaz of Ineos, and Nicolas Edet (Cofidis), Pello Bilbao (Bahrain McLaren), and wunderkind Marc Hirschi. From there, with numerical advantage, the Ineos pair got to work. Over the next seventy kilometres they formed a two-pronged instrument and slowly whittled the competition into an undignified pile of woodchip and shavings. With thirty to go they were clear, and we saw an entirely new Ineos form before our eyes. Living for the moment, racing for the day, just a couple of pals giving it full-gas off the front of the biggest bike race in the world.

It was beautiful: like a pair of lovely butterflies emerging from a tightly wrapped corporate chrysalis.

Back down the road, meanwhile, Richie Porte was busy scoffing a slice of his famous bad luck. The Montee du Plateau des Glieres, with it's steep, Sound-of-Music meadows, managed to conjure up a pesky stretch of gravel just beyond the summit; gravel, as we know, being the current road surface du jour. To see our neatly turned-out roadies negotiate it on their precision machines was a little undignified. Gravel requires thick tyres, cargo shorts, and ideally beards, in order to work. This was a kilometre and a half of please-god-don't-let-me-puncture! Jeopardy, judiciously placed by the race organisers.

Richie, of course, punctured. He skittered and bounced on airless rims. His hopes of a Tour podium hanging briefly in the balance. "No!" exclaimed the Tour bosses, watching on from their lair, committed Porte fans just like the rest of us, "we didn't mean to ruin Richie's race..."

That he would ultimately source a wheel change, chase back on, and lose no time, was testament to the fact that our favourite Tasmanian might just have found that against the odds survival instinct that has eluded and bedevilled him for so many years.

Meanwhile, Carapaz and Kwiatkowski, brothers-in-arms, hit the finishing straight in La Roche-sur-Foron. Alone. Just the two of them. All back slaps and cuddles, like a pair of lads on the final pint of a home town pub crawl. The humanity and shared joy enough to bring a tear to the eye. They had a little chat. Side-by-side, lingering, with love-heart emoji eyes, and crossed the line together. Bar the two-inch gap eeked-out surreptitiously by Kwiatkowski. A stage for him, a Polka-Dot jersey for his mate, and post-stage declarations of devotion all-round.

In a Tour that has had nothing whatsoever to do with team Ineos, Stage 18 was all about them. Just friends, on a cycling team, winning a bike race and giving us all a warm feeling in our collective tummy.

Standings after Stage 18

Yellow Jersey: Primoz Roglic

2nd Tadej Pogacar (+57 seconds)

3rd Miguel Angel Lopez (+1m 27 seconds)

Green (sprint/points): Sam Bennett

Polka Dots (mountains): Richard Carapaz

Stages 19-21: Drama!

19: randoms, renegades and variables

Be patient. Our Yellow Jersey grand finale is coming. Before that, Stage 19 would bring us a mixed bag of motivations and a slightly unhinged day of racing.

Tired legs; tough roads; teams without wins; riders with points to prove; and award-winning roast birds in the start town of Bourg-en-Bresse playing havoc with the finely calibrated calorie intake of several dozen hungry pro cyclists. These were the variables on the roads to Champagnole. While a ragtag gang of randoms and renegades raced, Roglic and Pogacar would sit tight for the crucial time trial on Stage 20.

And in amongst all this, Sam Bennett and Peter Sagan would hack away at each one last time in the search for Green Jersey points. The stage where Peter Sagan might salvage his – because it is normally his – annual prize. Only once since 2012 has he not won Green; 2017 being the year he was disqualified for an 'over-exuberant' sprint and Michael Matthews took the prize.

But Bennett, current wearer of green, was on the ball. Had he been subject to civilian rules in these pandemic-riven times he'd have been on the receiving end of one, long, continuous on-the-spot fine. He violated Sagan's personal space relentlessly for four solid hours. Neither social, nor distanced. On this rolling stage Sagan would need to take points at the intermediate sprint or bag a high placing at the finish to the detriment of his Irish shadow. But Bennett snuffed him out. Pointedly pipping him at each crucial moment. Asserting his right to tear that Jersey (politely and respectfully, of course), from the Slovakian's back.

Not only has Sagan not won a stage in this race he hasn't won so much as an intermediate sprint. His team have attacked, and hustled, and attempted to bully Bennett, to no avail. Without Sagan's relegation on Stage 11 for bullish sprint tactics the competition would have been tighter, and it's not mathematically over yet (because Paris, Stage 21), but right now Bennett looks like the clear winner.

Our squeaky-voiced superstar will not win Green this year.

In the final thirty kilometres, with the Yellow Jersey contenders looking on in wry, nowt-to-do-with-us-mate amusement, it was about the stage win. Which move would stick and by whom. With sixteen kilometres to go Stage 14 winner Soren Kragh Andersen sneaked out and around the vast Belgian torso of Tim Declerq (Deceuninck-Quickstep) and away. In the time it took us to recalibrate that part of our brain responsible for accepting that Kragh rhymes with 'cow' he was twenty seconds gone. Then thirty. And forty.

You get it. You understand how time works. This was our winner, that much we could see. Even if he couldn't. With a kilometre and a half to go he wheeled across to the camera moto and shouted, frantically, TIME?

TIIIME!!!

As in "excuse me my good man and/or woman...pray tell how far behind me the other chaps on bicycles are?" For a team who've shown us a great line in genius level bike racing tactics Sunweb seemed to be struggling to pass on the basic information that: "Soren, me old mate, you're well clear...enjoy yourself!"

Following his first stage win Kragh Anderson had admitted he wasn't sure he was up to the task. Now he's a double Tour de France stage winner. Career. Made.

Tomorrow comes the time-trail up the rather brilliant Planche des Belles Filles, a picturesque summit in Pinot (Thibaut...not noir) country. In another dimension this was to be Thibaut's coronation. Instead, while it's possible it will be Tadej Pogacar's it will probably be Primoz Roglic's.

20: Pogacar wins le tour...OMG!

Probably. I was hedging my bets to present the illusion of tension. Hinting at jeopardy despite the deal already being sealed. But what do I know? What to say? How to arrange the many words of the English language to accurately describe the sheer, lunatic surprise of Stage 20?

The idea that young Pogacar might overturn the fifty-seven second advantage of his countryman and pal? Pfffssshht! Suggest that, pre-stage, in polite company, and you'd have had your I-understand-pro-cycling badge revoked whilst your rear-end was handed to you on a corona-sanitised UCI branded plate.

Couldn't happen.

Wouldn't happen.

Happened.

The previous nineteen stages had been gripped tight, vice-like, by Roglic and his Jumbo Visma team. The Dutch outfit, for this race, had assembled a squad of such delicious talent around the most reliable, predictable, unshakeable team leader in the sport. Out Sky-ing Sky (not to mention Ineos), they had taken the process management of bike racing to a new level.

And yet, through hanging in, sometimes beating, and refusing to be truly dropped (see Stage 17 for the prime example of Pogacar fighting like a cornered mongoose to limit his losses), this implausibly young Slovenian (twenty-one, for goodness sake!) derailed the whole show with a mountain time trial up La Planche des Belles Filles for the ages. A triumph of improvised exuberance over stern control.

For the long rolling section of the thirty-five-kilometre course Roglic was down, slightly, against his rival. But he was still the winner of the 2020 Tour de France. He had time in hand. He's being cautious. He's judging effort. He's a consummate pro. Pogacar will fade.

These are the things we all said.

And then, at the base of La Planche, each rider took a bike change to swap from the aero machine onto the climbing bike. Pogacar remained sprightly, like a very skinny bunny picking up the scent of a particularly luscious patch of leafy greens. Roglic, at the same point, lost the plot. In the saddle, out of the saddle, wooden in style, helmet all askew, face pale.

Oh my god, we mouthed, collectively, as one, he's having a breakdown.

It was terrible to see.

Many of us had quite fancied the idea of Pogacar overhauling Roglic, not for anti-Roglic reasons but in the name of simple drama. But to see it happening, to watch a fellow human, on the brink of his dreams coming true, unravelling, was numbing. It felt polite to change TV channels and leave him in peace to be brutally mugged by his demons.

To seal the deal, Pogacar was on an absolute flyer. Devil-may-care, nothing-to-lose, time splits, after three and a half thousand kilometres, in his favour. Before we knew it, the Tour had done what the Tour sometime does. Flipped, in a split second, from one stone cold certain outcome to an entirely different one. Remain upright in Paris, tomorrow, and Tadej Pogacar has won the Tour de France.

Factor in a Lazarus-like third place finish for everyone's favourite bad luck story Richie Porte and we've only gone and found ourself, against the odds, a stone-cold classic.

Post-stage, teammates offered consoling hugs, but Roglic was elsewhere. Not in a mental place to receive a hug. A single bad day out of twenty and he's in the gutter.

21: it's not that easy being green

Tadej Pogacar is a selfish, selfish man. Not enough to deliver one of the greatest, most surprising comebacks the Tour de France has ever seen on Stage 20. Oh no. Yellow Jersey? Yep, I'll take that thanks...and I'll have the Polka Dots and that nice White one (best young rider) while I'm at it. The Green Jersey not to his liking, it seems.

Sam Bennett needed no second invitation. In nicking a couple of points at the intermediate sprint he sealed that deal. He now need only finish to win Green. We had the ramble into town; the laps around the Arc de Triomphe, down the Rue de Rivoli, and back up the Champs Elysees; and the slo-mo camera shots of golden sunlight and bike chains hopping and skipping on the cobbles.

Then we had the right left combo and the full-pelt finish of the unofficial sprinter's world championships. Mads Pederson (Trek Segafredo) showed off his rainbow bands, Peter Sagan bumped and barged, as he does, into contention, only for Bennett to brush them all off and win. Comprehensive. Deserved. To take Green and win the most coveted sprint in all of sprint-dom marking a coming-of-age for the emotional Irishman.

He held his Green bike aloft and roared the roar of a man who was in equal parts delighted to have won and relieved to have not let down his teammates; Deceuninck Quickstep having always struck me as a team where, if they work for you, you better damn well be a MAN and hold up your side of the bargain (not to mention your BIKE, for the CAMERAS!).

Paris, meanwhile, looked on with a Gallic, spectator-free shrug. Beckoning the helicopter camera to pan across her vista, to say: mais oui...Bennett is impressive impressive...but 'ave you seen 'ow pretty I look as the sun goes down. You should not be surprised. I am not London, after all, with its ridiculous penis buildings of glass and metal ...

We left her to continue the self-reverie and went in search of Tadej Pogacar. Totally Yellowed up – jersey, shorts, helmet, gloves, bar tape, shoes, bike – he strolled around and took the congratulations with nonchalance.

He finished the day as he began it: cool as a cucumber. He's either forgotten that he is now the youngest Tour winner in over a hundred years, or is laid-back with the certainty of a man who will win seven of the next nine and has the scribbled cure to Covid-19 on a hotel napkin in his jersey pocket having 'done the science' at the dinner table last night. Because nothing, right now, is beyond him. Except maybe the Green Jersey.

Tour de France Final Standings

Yellow Jersey: Tadej Pogacar

2nd Primoz Roglic (+59 seconds)

3rd Richie Porte (+3m 30 seconds)

Green (sprint/points): Sam Bennett

Polka Dots (mountains): Tadej Pogacar

Emmanuel Macron, the smoothly assured French President, is smart. Having laid the potential bear trap of le Tour de Covid-19 across his great country he would not step into it without first having a team of lackeys poke it with a stick. Trap duly un-triggered he appeared – smiling, waving, and sanitising furiously – on Stage 17, the absurdly challenging Queen Stage to the Col de la Loze.

Two-and-a-half weeks ago we struggled to imagine a public well behaved enough and a peloton sufficiently virus-free to allow the race to reach this outcome. It was the Tour with no finish line. Who could say at what point the weight of the public health machinery might step in and put the event out of its misery?

Stage 17 was the moment we knew. Our Tour de France would make it to Paris. Macron would simply not risk attaching his face to a failing endeavour, we reasoned. His presence was a sure sign. That Stage, I would argue, was also the moment when Tadej Pogacar won the Tour de France. I mean Stage 20 was when he won it, and technically Stage 21 was when he won it, won it, but the Col de la Loze was the inception.

It was painful to watch, over the mountainous Madeleine and up into the sky above Meribel. Team Jumbo Visma had gathered, mob-handed and menacing. On the highest slopes they launched their man Primoz Roglic to hunt down stage winner Lopez and Pogacar gave chase. Impossibly steep, little in the way of breathe-able oxygen, if a man's mental elastic band were ever to snap it would be here. Not fighting to overhaul his fellow Slovenian but to limit damage.

There would be no shame in losing a minute here. For Pogacar to limit the damage to a mere fifteen seconds in this intimidating, inhumane arena, with no teammates to help, against a rider in such control, was the foundation on which Stage 20 and la Planche was laid.

An alternative reading, glass half-empty, was that Jumbo Visma let Pogacar off the hook. Then, and on other occasions. For nineteen days, in dominantly shepherding Primoz Roglic to the very cusp of victory, they rode stupidly.

Stupidly.

You don't agree?

Take it up with Eddy Merckx. His words. In my current position, five-hundred and twenty-five pro victories in arrears of the great man, I don't feel qualified to interject. Because how would that go?

Eh, Eddy...you 'aven't got a clue mate

We all, except Eddy, saw Roglic going into that Stage 20 time-trial and winning the Tour. And he does have a point. Jumbo, dominant though they were, never did put the nail in Pogacar's coffin. A two-minute lead would have done it, but one? The coffin lid was ajar. The earth packed loosely above. The funeral was a rushed, complacent affair: pall bearers in un-ironed shirts; the hearse in need of a proper Turtle Wax; the organ requiring a tune-up. Enough for the funeral to take place, and no more.

This was not the clinical burial of a Team Sky in The Age of Froome. In fact, peak Team Sky would have cut the bullshit and opted for cremation. Quicker. Cleaner. Fewer variables.

But failings become glaring in hindsight. We should focus on Tadej Pogacar. His win was a triumph of grit, talent, and exuberance. A boyish face on a perfectly calibrated body, unencumbered by the weight of expectation, failure and regret; those triple pillars upon which the experience of a sporting life so often rests.

Rather than find fault we should celebrate the ability of the Tour de France to deliver the implausible. Make no mistake: as much as Primoz Roglic lost this race, and as much as Emmanuel Macron might like to claim some credit, Tadej Pogacar won it.

Giro d'Italia

Pre-Giro d'Italia, in the region of Emilia-Romagna, a lone camera operator in a helicopter is following each cyclist in turn along a hilly ridge. It is the World Championships, at Imola, and the organisers have stumbled upon the money shot. A long, tracking, viral clip. Each rider perched atop this great shoulder of Italian earth, the grace and majesty of the humble bicycle framed for a global TV audience.

And we are reminded what Italy is. What Italy does. What this complicated boot-shaped country is fundamentally all about. Hosting the UCI World Championships at short notice from a Covid-spooked Switzerland they managed to craft a beautiful, entertaining, hilly course for the reduced programme of events, and then make it look utterly gorgeous.

Because Italy, maybe more than any other place, is intensely visual. The way things look – the people, food, buildings and bikes – is central to their identity. The World Championships, sandwiched tightly between Tour and Giro, allowed us to reset. To say OK, now we're in Italy, the Tour de France is done and next comes the Giro.

Bumped from its usual slot in the calendar we would get an autumnal edition. The budding life and hopeful sunshine of May traded for the fluttering brown leaves of October. Daylight delivered in glancing blows. Still looking great, but brooding. And it would entertain, because it always does.

Our favourites for the race were a mixed bag. Grizzled veterans like Geraint Thomas, Vincenzo Nibali and Steven Kruijswijk; smooth skinned and beautifully groomed veterans like, well...Jakob Fuglsang, basically; and the ever-keen-as-mustard Simon Yates, a man who you sense will never live with his total-dominance-cum-utter-collapse in the 2018 Giro until he goes and wins the bloody thing.

And also, this being 2020, a crop of absurdly talented youngsters will emerge from nowhere and put the frighteners on the lot of 'em. In fact, probably win it. If twenty-one-year Tadej Pogacar can win the Tour de France then who knows what whipper snapper is about to follow suit here at the Giro.

Covid permitting, the Giro will deliver a dramatic and tension-filled #FightForPink (as the marketing men would have it). The hardest race in the most beautiful place.

Stages 1-4: Sicily

1: golden boy Ganna

And how better to start the Giro than with a home stage winner. Filippo Ganna (Ineos Grenadiers) has got the Midas touch. He's young, Italian and handsome. He's possessed of a lovely, lithe, flat-backed style on his (gold) bike. For the past week he's worn the rainbow bands of the time-trial World Champion (having powered his way, along that shoulder of earth, traced by that helicopter) and now, in his home Tour, he wears pink.

La Maglia Rosa.

The leader of the Giro.

The only low point in his life, according to reports, a total ban on Nutella at the Ineos Grenadiers breakfast table. Poor lad. That, right there, is sacrifice. He will surely change teams at the earliest opportunity.

Considering the calm control of young Pippo, this Stage 1 time-trial had unfolded in an atmosphere of scruffy chaos. This Giro, of course, had planned to roll out from Budapest, Hungary, but some virus or other put paid to those plans. Sicily stepped in at the last minute and threw together our opener. Hence, perhaps, a slightly wacky, scruffy, seat-of-the-pants fifteen-kilometre course. Sicily being a place that does a nice line in shabby chic. The slightly crumbling infrastructure and autumnal leaves swirling across a windswept finish line to add an atmosphere of edgy charm.

Starting in Monreale, the riders took in a steep kilometre of climbing before descending down long, straight roads interspersed with lumpy, bumpy, oil-slick hairpins. Into Palermo, a long and wind-battered way saw the riders home.

Some fell victim to the bumps and the lack of grip. Victor Campanearts (NTT Pro Cycling), the world hour record holder, hit the deck hard on a hairpin and finished his effort well back. Post-ride, he unfurled a shopping list of grievances in the direction of the first journalist to stick a microphone in his mush. Rohan Dennis (Ineos Grenadiers), Ganna's teammate, fell victim to the wind. The aero curves of his fancy bike gathering great gusts of weather and flicking him left and right across the road.

In between, others suffered to varying degrees. Conditions were pot luck. Ganna, clearly a man with fortune on his side, floated through unruffled.

For those with General Classification ambitions, keen on wearing the Pink Jersey after Stage 21 rather than Stage 1, it was a knife-edge situation. Simon Yates (Mitchelton-Scott), Jakob Fuglsang (Astana), Geraint Thomas (Ineos Grenadiers) and Steven Kruijswijk (Team Jumbo-Visma) had a fine line to pedal. Fast enough to avoid any early time losses, but slow enough to give you half a chance should the wind, or the Sicilian Tarmac, jump out and mug you.

Tense.

Miguel Angel Lopez (Astana), riding in support of his leader Fuglsang, offered a visceral reminder of the risk. At the nine-kilometre mark he switched his hands from aero bars to upright position on an innocuous section of flat road only for a pothole to snare his front wheel. The Colombian was thrown chest-akimbo across his bars and into the crash barriers. Brutally, Lopez's race concluded from the back of an ambulance.

Other losers were Lopez's leader Fuglsang and the man with coat hangers for shoulders Steven Kruijswijk, each losing well over a minute to Geraint Thomas. Thomas himself finishing almost within touching distance of golden-boy Ganna, with Simon Yates less than thirty seconds further back.

Some will now fling up arms declaring that for the likes of Kruijswijk and Fuglsang the race is gone. They'd do well to remember that for the Giro, the knife-edge is home territory. Stuff happens. Every year.

As for Ganna, now, he has two tasks at hand: Firstly, to convince me that his new nickname of Top Ganna (as in Tom Cruise) is a suitably witty moniker for such a talent, and secondly to convince boss Dave Brailsford that he's been a really good boy lately and that surely a dollop, just one, that's all, of that glorious chocolate spread, won't do any harm.

2: competition for eyeballs

After the shabby-chic of Stage 1, Sicily pulled out the best Sunday crockery. In this time-crunched coronavirus calendar the Giro bosses knew that up north, in Belgium, Liege-Bastogne-Liege was dealing up a schedule clash. The prestigious one-day classic offering serious competition for eyeballs. Fans would be tempted to watch Van der Poel, Alaphilippe, and Roglic do battle with the grim reality of a northern European autumn. Gritty, muscular racing, no doubt, but across a canvas of, well...Belgium.

Italy, as ever, has an answer to this. Into the southern Sicilian city of Agrigento the peloton passed the Valley of the Temples. A classic Giro trump card. The heart-aching beauty of a swathe of ancient architecture. Bathed in golden autumnal sunshine, a picturesque counterpoint to Liege's industrial estate glamour. A high-definition treat.

By happy consequence this was backed up by the Thomas-de-Gendt-is-in-the-break klaxon sounding loudly across social media. Our favourite bearded attacker was promising one of his miracle days, and viewers trickled south on a promise. An early hint that his form is better than at the recent Tour de France, where he attempted to sell his own legs on Twitter in frustration (no buyers!). Alas, it wasn't to be. The break was reeled in with ten kilometres to go. But consider yourself warned, peloton; De Gendt (Lotto-Soudal) is in the market for a Giro stage.

As for the gorgeous Stage 2 finish we had a steep, punchy ascent into the city. Could a climber surge clear? Could a fast finisher hang on and outsprint him? Could Peter Sagan (Bora-Hansgrohe) break his drought, after a winless Tour de France, and drag the attention of the entire pro cycling press south?

At the business end of the business end, Diego Ulissi (UAE Team

Emirates) proved as clinical as the Sicilian tourist board with a sniff of a Eurosport shop window. "I told Valerio Conti to accelerate to drop the sprinters on the last kilometre," he confirmed, post-stage, falling just short of a comedy throat slit 'kill them' gesture. His decisive teammate nailed it. "We were perfect, I'm really happy for this extraordinary success," Ulissi said. Not, it's fair to say, messing about.

Peter Sagan, meanwhile, clung and clambered up that climb and threatened, momentarily, to snag Ulissi. No doubt the Italian, had Sagan truly looked like catching him, would have instructed a teammate to deliver some other, equally brutal manoeuvre in the direction of everyone's favourite mammal. Sagan, in the end, fell short.

Behind the punchy finish the main contenders gathered in formation, while **golden-boy Ganna** retained pink. Two Italian wins in two stages. And tomorrow, the smouldering threat of Mount Etna.

Race Radio

Not all Sunshine and Birdsong

There are many ways to describe the Astana team leader Jakob Fuglsang. Silky, skinny, Danish. Veteran, too; at thirty-five you can count the number of opportunities he might have left to win a Grand Tour on one hand. Maybe even one finger.

This Giro was to be the one. In winning Il Lombardia, a monument of one-day cycling, back in August, he made a statement of intent. He also looked flippin' fantastic in doing so. Because he's that kind of rider. When he looks good, he looks so good: tall, lean, a picture of Scandinavian health. He has a perfectly coiffed head of hair and a fluid pedalling style that gives the impression of maximum power for minimum effort.

Following Lombardia he chose to forgo the Tour de France and threw all his carefully gathered eggs into one Italian basket. "I'm riding the Giro," he said, "and I'm taking my silky style and sheen of inevitable success with me."

And then, the Stage 1 time-trial, and my prediction politely resembled folly. He shipped a minute and a half to Ineos Grenadier and pre-race favourite Geraint Thomas. If that weren't enough his main man Miguel, world class climber and super-duper-domestique, careened into the roadside barriers to be carted off in an ambulance. To be followed, on Stage 2, by new main man Aleksander Vlasov heading home with stomach trouble. His team of mountain minders decimated in a blink.

But Stage 1 might have been an off day. And he can follow wheels and jump on board the mountain trains of other teams.

And for those Anglo Saxons amongst us who struggle with that mangled mouthful of a surname it translates, literally, as 'birdsong.'

And how can we not support a rider called Jacob Birdsong?

3: a bad day, a worse day, and a veteran's day

Often, late in a Grand Tour, you get those wild, ragged days in the mountains. Contenders and challengers are scattered, up and down the road; groups split into groups, re-form, and then split again; and Jerseys are sometimes won, and always lost. It's not often you get that as early as Stage 3.

Our mountain today was Etna. A summit which, every time it is raced, promises much - they're racing up a volcano, f'christ's sake – but often disappoints. The Etna of our imagination has the riders visible through smouldering embers; lava flows left and right; a rumble beneath the wheels, a suggestion of impending geological danger.

But a dull procession is always possible. Not hard enough, or neutralised by a headwind. Today the race took an intriguing route to the summit of the several options available. Three steep, high altitude kilometres would come into play, with riders softened up by the previous fifteen. There was a scent of drama (or was it sulphur?) in the air.

The day had begun whimsically. Race favourite Geraint Thomas took a tumble in the neutralised zone before the flag had formally dropped. We tutted, and chuckled, thinking nothing of the (apparently) superficial damage to kit and pride. As the race came within full sight of the slopes of Etna we saw immediately, shockingly quickly, that there was nothing funny about this. Thomas slid back through the peloton, and then off the back, and away out of contention. Grimacing, in discomfort, and unable to put power through the pedals.

"This is now difficult to watch," commented Bradley Wiggins, solemnly, on Eurosport, Thomas being a rider known to endure hardship more successfully than most. He was in a bad way and his Giro, at least the Pink part of it, done. Simon Yates, by default, the new race favourite.

A few kilometres up the road and the pace was quickening. Vincenzo Nibali (Trek-Segafredo), the Sicilian on his home volcano (and how many rides can say that) had put his teammates to work on the front. They had an ulterior motive. Because where is Yates? And what in God's name is going on here! Off the back, paced by teammates, and unable to ride in the wheels. Another victim.

Yates reached the summit three minutes behind the leaders. Not quite the sporting disaster that befell the Ineos man (Thomas was a further nine minutes back) but, in the understated words of Mitchelton-Scott team boss and uber-Aussie Matt White, "a bad day."

Or, to be more accurate (and also Aussie): "ahhh, look mate...it's a bad day."

All of which utter madness left the veterans on parade. Nibali, Fuglsang, Pozzovivo (NTT Pro Cycling) and Kruijswijk the strongest of the GC contenders through the atmospheric gloom befitting of the top of a massive volcano. All having now manoeuvred themselves into threatening top ten positions. In pink is Portuguese rider Joao Almeida (Deceuninck-Quickstep), capitalising on a strong Stage 1 time-trail to deliver a solid summit finish. On a day for the old guys, the twenty-two-year-old reminded us that 2020 is all about the kids.

Which brings us to the Stage winner, Jonathan Caicedo (EF Pro

Cycling). The Ecuadorian, after labouring away in a presumed doomed breakaway all day, found deep reserves of strength on those upper slopes. Having long since left his colleagues behind the miniature climber, short and stocky, the apparent result of an experiment to fuse the DNA of Nairo Quintana (Arkea-Samsic) and Domenico Pozzovivo, nailed it.

Let's all agree that this Giro, only three stages in, is bonkers, and random, and highly unpredictable. The only sensible course of action now to stop second guessing, sit back, and let it unfold.

Race Radio

Fast Fashion

The eight-man breakaway on Stage 3 was a catwalk. A study in 2020 pro-cycling style. We had Giovanni Visconti resplendent in the teal blue/yellow flouro of Italian outfit Vini Zabu-KTM. Sponsor heavy, quintessentially Italian, and looking the absolute business, but unable to hold a candle to Lawson Craddock and Jonathan Caicedo of EF Pro Cycling.

Unwilling to countenance a clash between their standard pink livery and the might of the Maglia Rosa – the Pink Jersey reserved for the race leader – for this race EF came up with an away kit. Their respect for tradition to the fore. The convenient fact of a massive marketing exercise nothing more than an afterthought, of course.

EF, it's fair to say, went left field. So far left field as to employ a skateboard brand (Palace) to work with their usual kit supplier (Rapha) and under strict instructions to push the boat out. Go wild. Stick a weird optical illusion pattern in there.

Flames on the sleeves? Yes please. Add a duck, if you like. Unsurprisingly, they monopolised the pre-Giro kit coverage.

We had thought that Trump v Biden, Left v Right, and Brexit v Remain were the societal issues dividing Western civilisation down the middle in 2020. Now we have the new EF kit. There is no fence sit on here.

Caicedo, in winning Stage 3, blew the collective mind of the uber-conservative pro cycling establishment with his highly hastaggable attire. The days of crisp minimalism may be on the way out. I, along with exactly 50% of Western civilisation, am here for it.

4: reverse-Samson and the curse of Cofidis

It was a tale of four sprinters. Also, one fewer Pink Jersey contender; Geraint Thomas having bailed out with yesterday's, as it turned out, fractured pelvis. As excuses go, it's good.

Stage 4 ran from Catania to Villafranca, our final day in Sicily before a mainland pilgrimage, and featured a single category three climb,

Portella Mandrazzi, slap bang in the middle. Whichever sprinters ascended this obstacle in contact with the main field would gather for a bunch sprint finish. Fernando Gaviria (UAE Team Emirates), a man who favours a pan-flat parcours, was very much up against it.

And I have to point out that, at some point in the last few years the Colombian got hairy. Really hairy. Thick brown locks now flow luxuriously from his helmet, he has the densely stubbled chin of a Canadian lumberjack, and he wins less. He's getting slower. It's a clear case of reverse-Samson; while that biblical hero of the Israelites drew power from his hair Gaviria grows weaker with every additional inch upon his head. Having said that, he's never been a man for the hills, though. He could've shaved himself bald as a coot for today's race and still struggled.

With the climb done, and Gaviria duly dropped, the teams of the other three key sprinters - Sagan, Viviani (Cofidis) and Demare (Groupama-FDJ) - hit the front and drilled it; because even a hairy Gaviria is a threat in a sprint. Better that he be cut loose decisively and dispatched before it came to that.

Peter Sagan had cleared the mountain with ease. Having not won a bike race since early 2019 he lived in hope that his mojo was awaiting discovery somewhere on the descent. He's searched high and low across most of the rest of Europe, so who knows? Worth a look.

Elia Viviani has also misplaced his killer instinct. Having left Deceuninck Quickstep at the end of 2019 as one of the world's premier sprinters, he hasn't won a race since. As we often see, any rider to leave that all-conquering team immediately becomes somewhat less-conquering. Or perhaps it's the curse of Cofidis; you join the French squad and you immediately inherit their inability to win.

Which left his countryman Arnaud Demare. Confident, resplendent in the Tricolore, winner in 2020 of the French National Championships, Milan-Torino, and a small flock of other races in this truncated season. Call it a mojo, a killer instinct, or even a lucky streak, he knows where it is and isn't afraid to use it.

With teammates in full formation, like a French TGV rattling unstoppably through a provincial station, Demare was the final carriage on a good old-fashioned lead-out train through the streets of Villafrance. Riders peeled off. Sagan hopped from wheel to wheel. Viviani floated, innocuously, never quite there. Head-to-head, neck and neck, Sagan and Demare, a dive for the line and a photo finish.

And it's the Frenchman by a tyre tread. To shrugs, and eyebrows raised, and "I dunno...did I get it?" Ten more psi in his tyres and Sagan might've won.

Standings after Stage 4

Pink Jersey: Joao Almeida

2nd Jonathan Caicedo (+2 seconds)

3rd Pello Bilbao (+39 seconds)

Cyclamen (sprint/points): Peter Sagan

Blue (mountains): Jonathan Caicedo

Stages 5-7: Toe to Heel

5: crash Pippo...CRASH!

At the summit of Montescuro the Giro - this autumnal, late-season edition – pulled out it's bag of tricks. The drama-o-meter cranked up to five.

Thick fog hung across the Tarmac, clinging to the trees like dry-ice billowing about the legs of a power balladeer. The late afternoon gloom had riders illuminated by moto headlights, legs shining in the rain, for added drama. And as if that weren't enough, the man to crest the top and attack the descent first was Filippo Ganna.

Implausible, far-fetched, but true.

Stage 1 winner, Italian hero, and a track cyclist with no business leading a bike race through these southern, Calabrian mountains. When he rides on the road, he wins time trials. He is not man for the gritty arm-wrestle of a weather-beaten mountain stage. He is an aerodynamic, variable levelling control-freak.

Or, maybe, as social media is suggesting, he's the new Miguel Indurain?

(Too soon, but ok...we'll see.)

Sure, he was in the break, and that was within the realms of possibility, but he was there as teammate and helper for Salvatore Puccio (Ineos Grenadiers) and cannon fodder for king-of-the-breakaways Thomas de Gendt. Until deep into the twenty-five-kilometre ascent of our final summit when he reinvented himself as free-spirited mountain escapee, riding away from De Gendt and Einar Rubio (Movistar Team), the climbing Colombian youngster, and into the distance.

When he crested Montescuro he had fifty-seconds on the peloton and several kilometres of treacherous descent between him and the finish. He also had super-descender Vincenzo Nibali, chasing him, to think about. Passing between clouds, in and out of the fog, and with rain drumming ever more heavily against his broad, flat back, jeopardy hung in the air.

So close to the win, desperate to keep the bunch at bay, we watched his wheels around each bend for the lurching twitch that would send him into a barrier. Things could still go very wrong. Brian Smith, on Eurosport, in that former Directeur-Sportif manner of his, assured us that: "he's got this...they'll not catch him now."

Affecting an air of calm, he was reassuring himself. Managing his own nerves. The rain, the dark, the fog, we thought, to see him crashing here requires no leap of imagination whatsoever...In fact, the quicker he crashes the better, to put us out of our misery.

CRASH Pippo...CRASH, f'christs sake!

But he didn't. Because he's the golden boy and this is his time. He's doing that thing that cyclists (and sportspeople) in form sometimes do. He's bending the narrative, even the very concept of plausibility, to his will. He took the win by a comfortable thirty-four seconds. Ganna has now won forty-percent of all the Grand Tour stages he has ridden (two out of five). Italians have won sixty percent of this Giro to date. Forza Italia!

He is a track cyclist who might, just might, be reinventing himself as a Grand Tour rider before our very eyes. We've seen Ineos (neé Sky) develop riders like this before. Should Ganna now cultivate a set of luxurious Wiggins-esque lambchop sideburns and reveal an eye-catching line in caustic media wit we will watch with interest.

Race Radio

Put the Boot In

Being boot-shaped is an often-overlooked reason why Italy is so well suited to host a three-week bike race. It's basic geography. With Paris Roubaix, or Liege Bastogne Liege, for example, the logistics are obvious. We check in with these races each year, and give or take the odd twist or turn through some newly favoured (or, ahem, deep-pocketed) town en route, we know the plan.

Start in Liege, ride to Bastogne, and back again. Once you have a rough idea of where these places are you have a sense of the race. They don't move.

But take Stage 5, from Mileto to Camigliatello Silano. Could you really, hand on heart, locate this on a map? But what if I told you the route ran along the top of the foot of Italy? The metatarsal, if you like. Now you know where we are.

Tomorrow, Stage 6, traverses the sole in the direction of the heel. From there we will visit the heel itself, before sliding seductively up the calf, with a quick detour into the ankle, before heading to the mountains at the top of the boot.

This doesn't work with the Tour de France. They describe their country as a hexagon, but have you ever tried to describe your location in terms of a hexagon?

Italy, boot-shaped, is made for bike racing.

6: sacre bleu, mon Dieu, etc.

With fifteen kilometres to go on a likely sprinter's stage, Eurosport like to cut to everyone's favourite Austrian: Bernie Eisel. As a recent former pro, 'handsome Bernie' is well placed to talk us through the finish as the riders approach it. But he describes, and explains, and clarifies, in that weird generic Euro-speak of his, and we glaze over. As when you pull over a passer-by and ask for directions, only a tiny amount of the information seeps in. The rest is merely air molecules passing across ear drum.

Yeah, nice one...cheers mate! you say, before wandering off to follow your nose and take pot-luck.

The way he explained the run-in to Matera today, on Stage 6, you'd have been forgiven for thinking the final three kilometres consisted of a maze, through which the riders must navigate, blindfolded, with the single exit leading out to a secret finish line.

Up. Down. Flat for a bit. Into town. Right, left, right. Finishing straight.

Ok. Thanks Bernie.

The city of Matera, in the Basilicata region, when it revealed itself, was a thing of utter beauty. With religious buildings perched upon cliffs; dug-out dwellings carved into the rock beneath; staircases, wending lanes, and a rocky ravine winding by. One of the oldest continuously inhabited settlements in the world, no less. It seemed churlish to sully its beauty with something so noisy and chaotic as a bike race.

Clearly the race organisers agreed. For much of the last ten kilometres, as the helicopter gave us sweeping views, the peloton skirted the town, barrelling around a wide-laned ring-road. Nowhere near anything beautiful. I suppose, to be fair, rocky outcrops and prehistoric staircases are not the ideal terrain for a road race.

Many of us had today, 8th October 2020, as the day when Peter Sagan would break The Big Drought. July 2019 was his last win. Today's sprint stage featured an awful lot of hills, with a particularly steep one in the final couple of kilometres. He would hang on to the punchy climbers before outsprinting them for the win. It would be like Stage 2 but this time he would beat Ulissi (or whoever) rather than vice-versa. And up until the final few hundred metres it went to script.

We pulled on our comedy fake goatees and gave it full squeaky voice in honour of the big moment only to watch, alarmed, a he mistimed a move, and then another, and slid back and out of contention.

Arnaud Demare, meanwhile, having hovered around twentieth place well into the last kilometres, apparently taking a little breather, took the final left-hander (you know, the one Bernie mentioned) and glided at enormous speed around, past, and through everyone to win by a country mile. Sacre bleu! Mon Dieu! And other cliched French exclamations. Our disappointment at Sagan's defeat trumped by the sheer glory of Demare's long range effort. A phenomenal win.

The ancient city looked on. Unmoved. Paleolithic. A visit from the Giro just another event in its long history. We could make jokes about the time-span since Sagan's last win, but let's just say allez Demare!

7: the road to Brindisi

With enough imagination, "The Road to Brindisi" could be the title of a Booker nominated novel. Penned by some giant of literary fiction. A modern tale of love and loss across the plains of Italy.

"A triumph!" The Evening Standard.

"Un-putdownable!" Stephen Fry.

"Not as easy as I'm making it look!" Arnaud Demare.

Our finish in this historic Adriatic trading city, in contrast to yesterday's Bernie Eisel described riddle, was simple. A sharp right turn into a dead-flat, arrow-straight kilometre. The sprinters would unfurl their mighty sprints. The fastest man would win. Nothing to it. Right?

Well, maybe. But only with a strong team at your service. Early in the stage the ranks of Deceuninck Quickstep and Jumbo Visma were marshalled in support of race leader Joao Almeida and Dutch contender Steven Kruijswijk. Sensing the jeopardy of crosswinds, they were put to work in protection of their precious cargo. If only the road had been washed with sideways rain and slathered with Belgian cowshit they'd have been in heaven. Because these northern European teams LOVE a mucky fight in a crosswind.

They gathered at the front, a quick check that all were present and correct, and then BOSH! An acceleration. The race was rent asunder. Groups of riders up and down the road. Crashes. Mild panic. Kruijswijk and Almeida safely at the front, other riders with strong teammates – Demare, Nibali, Sagan - there too. The unlucky ones left exposed.

With thirty kilometres remaining the peloton was in thirds. It would come together, eventually, for our finish, but damage had been done. Pity a guy like Elia Viviani. The Italian sprinter, without a win all season, could, on a stress-free day, challenge Demare and Sagan. But after a lengthy brawl for position and an energy sapping game of catch-up into town? No chance. His Cofidis team lacked the muscle to protect their man.

While Viviani was fighting, the other two were in the care of their trusty chaperones. Nudging, elbowing, and battling for position. Demare, delivered, for the final surge, found our favourite Slovak slap bang on his wheel. Yes Peter, we whispered. We believed. We dwelt briefly on how sinister it sounds to whisper Yes Peter to no-one in particular and then we waited. The strands of our story were coming together. We have nothing against Arnaud Demare but we want a Sagan win. We've waited long enough (July 2019, need I remind you). Our man would leap from Demare's wheel to take it. We knew he would. A couple of twists and turns. A final right-angle into the finish. Would Sagan dive right along the barriers, or left and around?

Come OOONNNN Peter! we roared, less sinister now, committed.

But Demare is a force. It's tempting to imagine the 'old' Sagan would've brushed him aside but what use is that? Right now, in this Giro, Arnaud Demare is unbeatable in a sprint. A hilly one. A flat one. A windy one. It makes little difference.

"The Road to Brindisi" was a tale of love and loss. The hero of the story was, yet again, for the third time in seven stages, a big blonde Frenchman.   And   Sagan   was   powerless   to   resist.

Standings after Stage 7

Pink Jersey: Joao Almeida

2nd Pello Bilbao (+43 seconds)

3rd Wilko Kelderman (+48 seconds)

Cyclamen (sprint/points): Arnaud Demare

Blue (mountains): Filippo Ganna

Race Radio

Pristine in Pink

Joao Almeida, tanned, composed and unruffled, is our pristine race-leader. Twenty-two years old. Neat and tidy on the bike, poker faced and self-contained. His progress since acquiring the Pink Jersey on Stage 3 has been serene.

He has a face too young to display the grizzled markings of his profession. Close inspection suggests a strict regime of exfoliation and moisturisation. Being a millennial, see, he is probably not averse to a spot of male grooming. And he has the tan. The deep, even, Portuguese bronze.

He's the very epitome of the classy young European pro.

His list of achievements, in this young career, is replete with junior-this and under-23 that. A super-talented kid who finds himself in the lead of one of the world's biggest bike races. But that's not quite fair. He doesn't 'find himself' anywhere, he has positioned himself cleverly to seize Pink. A superb opening day time-trial, a strong finish on Etna on Stage 3, e voilà!

But we are yet to enter the highest mountains. He has a strong team

(Deceuninck Quickstep) working hard to support him but there'll come a point when he will have to fend off attacks and suffer the face-creasing pain of defending a leader's jersey. We will discover the strength of both his legs and his face cream.

On the one hand it's almost impossible to imagine him actually winning the Giro d'Italia. On the other, this is 2020, and yawn...almost getting boring now...extravagantly talented young cyclists...blah-de-blah...

If nothing else, the kid looks born to do it.

Stages 8-10: Northbound

8: destination of choice for Dowsett

On Stage 8, the message from the Giro was clear: at ease people, take a day off. We know you're sick of coronavirus, we all are, so here are some suggestions. A curated brochure if you like, for a wonderful, sun-kissed holiday next year when all this has blown over.

While precisely nothing happened in the race the TV helicopter took us off on rambling tours of the surroundings. The Gargano National Park, the spur on the heel of Italy, looked so inviting. The emerald green waters of the Adriatic lapped gently against hidden coves, secret beaches and tucked-away villas where who knows who might get up to god knows what.

Drug dealing?

Diamond smuggling?

Really high-quality socialising?

We saw yachts and pleasure cruisers, and cursed the good fortune of those on board as they sipped a crisp glass of something and baked in the beauty of their surroundings. That shall be me next year, we thought, as one. Our new holiday destination of choice.

Coronavirus, of course, being on our mind following overnight news of a positive test for Simon Yates and his withdrawal from the race. Explaining, at a stroke, his poor form in this race. The first rider to exit a Grand Tour in that fashion. Probably not the last.

With seventy kilometres to go today, and a ten-minute lead, that the winner would come from our breakaway group was in no doubt. These six plucky riders had chosen to put in a ferocious shift while the peloton meandered. The sawtooth profile of the day's stage guaranteeing barely a flat metre of road all day.

Of that six we had two British riders: Matt Holmes (Lotto-Soudal), from Wigan, home of pies, rugby league, and straightforward opinion, and Alex Dowsett (Israel Start-up Nation), the Essex time-trail specialist. Of the two, he's the guy with the bike race winning pedigree. Dowsett has won many a high-profile TT over the years. Could he really take a Giro road stage? If he could, it would be the first Grand Tour stage for team Israel Start-up Nation (weird team name, let's be honest...). He would write his name in their history. The origin story to whatever might come next. He's also riding without a contract for 2021, and so what better way to nudge his employees in the ribs and give them the come-hither eyes?

Into Vieste and the finishing circuit, tired legs were in evidence. The unrelenting terrain of the day ensuring that attacks were lumbering and unable to stick. When Salvatore Puccio (Ineos Grenadiers) and Matt Holmes eventually dragged their weary limbs clear on the steep circuit climb that looked, momentarily, like it.

But Dowsett, highly motivated by his impending unemployment, was shepherded back to the leaders by a final effort from his teammate Matthias Brandle (Israel Start-up Nation). He then attacked, with that sustained power so befitting his muscular frame, and that really was it. Dowsett gathered enough time to insulate himself from Holmes and Puccio on the second go up the climb, and from there his win was sealed.

Into the finish, well clear, he swerved briefly around a random three-legged dog. He looked tired, emotional, and very happy indeed (Dowsett, that is, not the dog). Post-stage revelations of his impending fatherhood, and his understandable desire to put food on the table for the new addition, bringing the precariousness of pro sport into sharp focus. And so, it's back to the hotel, quick shower, and a knock on his bosses bedroom door to just gimme' the damn contract already!

9: Vincenzo's vigil

Sowing the seeds of doubt, uncertainty, anxiety and indecision. That has been the modus operandi of Vincenzo Nibali and his team to date in this Giro d'Italia. Without doing anything to definitively suggest he is the strongest General Classification rider he has convinced many of us that he's the favourite. His Trek-Segafredo team, of course, have been highly visible. One of only two or three teams who look capable of controlling a bike race, they have been front and centre at key moments. But more than this, Nibali, the wily veteran, has nipped to the front to make a point from time to time.

At moments of peril, not when you would expect an attack but when the peloton is strung out and really rattling along, through winding village streets or on a quick descent, he has appeared. We've edged our collective buttocks toward the lip of our seats, quizzically, to ask: Nibali...eh? What's this?

Once he's elbowed himself into our (and his rivals) consciousness he eases back and hides again. Point made. Old Nibbles is looking good, we think, without thinking, and this becomes the truth of it. Just how good he is, we don't yet know.

Today might've been the day when he made a bid for Pink, for the simple reason that (you might have heard) there's a virus knocking around and we can't be sure the race will make it to Milan. If our Giro is cut short, and we have a winner-by-default situation on our hands, it would surely be handy to find yourself in possession of the Pink Jersey when those questions are being asked. Also, today was a mountainous one, and tomorrow is a rest day.

The complication of Stage 9 was the truly miserable conditions. Rain, wind, single figures cold. Jackets were on and off. Faces were set and grim. Survival was job number one. Nibali, of course, was short-sleeved all day. Probably for all the reasons explained above. It's part of the show. He is also known to endure cold and bad weather like an ancient stoic.

On occasions his team came to the front and upped the pace, the peloton on tenterhooks at the imminent full-scale attack. There was tension and nervousness. Rivals coiled, like springs, burning mental energy as well as physical in the anticipation of the moment that was imminent. And then Trek would melt away. Take stock. Look into the eyes of rivals and ask questions that went beyond mere words. It's almost, dare I say, as if he isn't actually as strong as he'd have us believe.

Approaching the final (of many) climbs, the steady ten kilometres to the summit at Roccaraso, the break of five hardy, suffering souls – Warbasse (AG2r La Mondiale), Bjerg (UAE Team Emirates), Guerrero (EF Pro Cycling), Frankiny (Groupama-FDJ) and Castroviejo (Ineos Grenadiers) – were clear and would win the day. Nibali, we knew, would launch from the group of favourites behind in search of time gains. He stalked Pink Jersey Joao Almeida like, well…a veteran Italian cyclist on the tail of a plucky Portuguese kid.

For the win, it was Ruben Guerrero and Jonathan Castroviejo who stretched clear in the final few kilometres and treated us to an agonising, bike-wrenching slo-mo 'sprint' on the final 12% ramps. The moment when Castroviejo cracked, head slumped, limbs turned to rubber, was cruel. Guerrero dragged himself to the line ten metres clear and pointed to himself repeatedly and with great aggression. "Me," we can only assume he was saying, "me won!!"

And back down the road Nibali waited, and hovered, and loitered, and lingered, before crossing the line and losing a tiny handful of seconds to rivals Fuglsang and Wilko Kelderman (Team Sunweb). No attack. Nothing doing. Almeida still in Pink. As you were chaps. And with that, Nibali continues his intriguing vigil in our collective head.

10: Peter Sagan is glorious, ridiculous and barely possible

Current mood: uncertain. Governments the length and breadth of the continent, with a dubious mix of foresight, hindsight, and blind faith, are responding to a current wave of coronavirus infections. A bike race, in his context, and depending on your view, is either a welcome distraction or a public health disaster. Teams are making decisions.

Simon Yates abandoned last week after testing positive. The post-rest day news was of the withdrawal of his entire Mitchelton-Scott team following further positives in the team bubble. Steven Kruijswijk, of Team Jumbo Visma, announced a positive pre-Stage 10 and his team also followed suit. Mass withdrawals. The peloton thinning before our eyes.

Those of who choose to engage in the mental-health black-spot known as Twitter waited this morning with a sense of doom, for more news. Other positive tests? Further team withdrawals? A collapse of the entire Giro and a win by default for Vincenzo Nibali via some kind of Italo-centric algorithmic countback? Surprisingly, the only further pre-stage announcement concerned Michael Matthews (Team Sunweb) testing positive, heading off home, but leaving the remainder of the team intact and in the race. The wisdom of that decision will reveal itself in the coming days.

As for Stage 10, between Lanciano and Tortereto, the saw-tooth profile promised a muscular, punchy kind of a race. Man-of-the-people Peter Sagan, understanding that the world needs cheering up, hatched a plan to get in the breakaway. After an initial hundred kilometres of hell-for-leather the peloton gave up the chase and let him go clear with Filippo Ganna, Ben Swift (Ineos Grenadiers), Dario Cataldo (Movistar Team) and others. On the hunt for sprint points and an implausible all-day breakaway stage win.

The climbs en route rose like walls. Fifteen and twenty percent, one after another. Leg sapping. The heavens opened so that slippery roads might add a sprinkling of jeopardy. Sagan was resolute on the front, dropping companions one-by-one, and slowly, climb-by-climb, we began to wonder. We edged closer to the telly and WhatsApp'd our mates to drop whatever pretence at a 'day's work' they were currently engaged in and find a TV screen. Into the final twenty kilometres and Sagan dispatched Ben Swift, the last man able to hang on to his skin-tight coat tails. He was now alone.

Behind, an ever-reduced peloton still assumed they would catch him. Diego Ulissi fancied the stage win and put his team to work. Domenico Pozzovivo, the tiny veteran, fancied the Pink Jersey and put himself to work. Joao Almeida, already in Pink, ran out of teammates and fought like a beautifully tanned, highly composed dog, to keep it. Pello Bilbao (Bahrain-McLaren) nipped off the front and then got caught again. Wilko Kelderman and Vincenzo Nibali hung around and stayed safe. Jakob Fuglsang drew the short straw, puncturing late to lose a minute and more.

The gap reduced. The margins tightened. And Peter Sagan was still clear.

You just knew, from kilometre zero, that his breakaway

companions had bemoaned his presence in that group. They understood they would be given nothing. Arnaud Demare's team would chase them to defend the sprinters jersey. An understanding within the group that Sagan was the fast finisher would kill any desire for the break to succeed as one. This was not a motivated, cohesive effort. It was Sagan v The World. Ride this race, with this context, a hundred times, and Sagan would win from that break on half of one occasion. So unlikely as to be statistically confusing.

With each new wall scaled and his companions long since cast to the wind he carried a lead of teens-of-seconds, for ten kilometres, into the town of Torttereto. The clock flickering, threatening to plunge to a catch, but resisting. A long finishing straight. The sun, unable to contain itself, burst through the rain. A rainbow appeared (really!).

A gentle, wry, remember-me? salute.

A glorious, ridiculous, beautiful, barely possible Peter Sagan win.

If the Giro packs up tomorrow in deference to the coronavirus, no matter. We've had our money's worth. Peter Sagan is once more the greatest pro cyclist on the planet.

Standings after Stage 10

Pink Jersey: Joao Almeida

2nd Wilko Kelderman (+34 seconds)

3rd Pello Bilbao (+43 seconds)

Cyclamen (sprint/points): Arnaud Demare

Blue (mountains): Ruben Guerreiro

Stages 11-13: Coastal Towns and Covid-anxiety

11: Demare hits the dance-floors of Rimini

A quiet day. A trough to the screaming peak of Stage 10. A day of slo-mo- replays of inconsequential activity; the flap of a gilet in the wind, a drip of moisture from the tip of a cyclist's nose. A ho-hum day to add texture to a three-week bike race.

You know the kind of thing. A rider leans over to visibly chat with another and the helicopter camera zooms in to capture the moment. Glad of anything vaguely eye-catching to pass a kilometre or two. "Peter Sagan there," our commentary team confirm, "no doubt just fine-tuning tactics with his team mate." Or, y'know, reminiscing about that big, messy night out in Rimini back in 2015. The Adriatic resort being our finish today for the absolute stone-cold certainty of a bunch sprint finish.

The doomed breakaway, five Italians and a Belgian, perhaps chose their fate to simply avoid any peloton related Covid-transmission for another day. Not seeking to win but simply stay healthy.

Until the twisty town-centre finish only Italian sprinter Elia

Viviani, desperate for a win, found reason for alarm. With thirty kilometres to go, peeling right at a roundabout, an in-race moto attempted to slip past the bunch. Clipping Viviani's wheel, he was sprawled, undignified; as if having to race in that basic red/white/yellow Cofidis skinsuit – surely designed by a child – weren't enough, he found himself splayed, legs akimbo, and with stage favourite Arnaud Demare rattling away up the road. He would chase back on but wouldn't contest the sprint. Even such a mild-mannered chap as Viviani surely spitting (strictly within the team bubble, you understand, for safety reasons) feathers at such unnecessary drama.

Into Rimini, the peloton negotiated the infrastructure of the biggest party town on the Adriatic coast with aplomb. First Israel Start-up Nation, then Team UAE, bossed it. Their sprinters Rick Zabel and Fernando Gaviria feeling presumably perky. Sagan, as he does, wheel-surfed serenely. And then with two kilometres to go Demare's team – big, and muscular – simply shrugged them all aside. Any nearer to the Rimini beach and they'd have kicked sand in the eyes of their rivals and stolen their girlfriends. In a town undoubtedly well-versed in a peacock display of Alpha-dominance it was comprehensive.

"Hard luck lads," they said, "Arnaud's coming through."

Demare cruised to the front. Gaviria accelerated, now clearly in the grip of a full reverse-Samson situation, and may have literally stopped and gone backwards so far off the pace was he. Sagan, legs surely tired from his glorious Stage 10 exploits, wrestled and wrangled, but the French sprinter was again untouchable. The winner now of four of this race's eleven stages. That's 36.4% of the Giro to date, percentage fans.

Were we not in corona-times he'd surely be out cutting some rug on the dancefloors of Rimini tonight. He'll have to settle for Covid-safe celebration in the team bubble. It's another day ticked off for Pink Jersey Almeida (that's eight now), and another day closer to Milan. Whether this Giro, pandemic 'n' all, gets that far, feels somewhat in the balance.

12: you are now entering Pantani country

Stage 12, and this is Marco Pantani territory. The roads are scrawled with his name – not just today, but always; the reverence people from this area have for the man is palpable. It's emotional. Whatever your view on Pantani you cannot ignore his deep place in their lives.

It also, judging by the cardiograph stage profile, looked like Thomas de Gendt territory. But a single morning Tweet from our favourite Belgian escape artist said otherwise: "I don't feel like racing today, the situation is trending the wrong direction and it feels like the organiser conceals things. We're having discussions between riders whether we should start."

He's talking coronavirus (as most of us are). Clearly not got his attack-the-race-with-reckless-abandon head (or legs) on. The daily mutterings from riders now do not bode well. Milan should probably put a pause on inflating all those Pink balloons and hang fire on the massive pink lighting rig at the Duomo di Milano. The party is in the balance.

Four hours into today's five-and-a-half-hour stage much of the peloton might happily have climbed off, race abandoned, let's find the nearest hot shower. Conditions were atrocious. Bitterly cold, driving wind and rain, glassy roads; it was appalling. For a cyclist, tough to watch. Few of us can relate to the experience of riding a Giro, but many of us have experienced a truly wet and cold day on the bike. To see the mighty Vincenzo Nibali swinging his arms like a rank amateur in search of blood flow was truly a great leveller.

With still fifty kilometres to go the break was well clear, itself in dribs and drabs, while a reduced peloton saw Nibali and Jakob Fuglsang teammate-free. Forced to ferry back and forth to their own team car in search of warm drinks, clothing, and perhaps a kind word from an empathetic Directeur Sportif. Wilko Kelderman and Domenico Pozzovivo, also contending for Pink, each had a rag-tag of teammates on hand.

Only Pink Jersey Joao Almeida had a genuinely strong band of lieutenants in his service: Peter Serry, James Knox, and Fausto Masnada (all Deceuninck-Quickstep) would remain heroically with their leader to the bitter end at the finish in Pantani's town, Cesenatico. Almeida's ever-composed face set in a frozen grimace. Thoughts of attack from any of the team leaders totally neutralised on a day of simple survival.

Up the road, into the final twenty, we had Jhonatan Narvaez (Ineos Grenadiers) and Marc Padun (Bahrain McLaren). Soaked to the skin, frozen to their core, and in search of the biggest win of their fledgeling careers. Either able to keep warm(ish) by the fact of riding hard in the break all day or simply made of tougher stuff than you, me, and a peloton of the finest (and, crucially in this weather, skinniest) athletes on the planet.

To see Padun puncture in the final stages, watch Narvaez ride off down the road, procure a new wheel, chase him, and get within nine measly seconds before finally cracking was, for we viewers, not something to be enjoyed as much as endured. On balance, and young though he is, I imagine Padun has also had more enjoyable half-hours.

As for Narvaez, regardless of Padun's bad luck you cannot deny the man his win on a day like today. A first Grand Tour stage win and a special issue 'I've been a tough-guy' badge to sew onto his Ineos shorts. As for the race? The coronavirus? The Italian Public Heath apparatus? Thomas de Gendt's state of mind?

Who knows?

We must enioy this Giro, and sometimes endure it, one day at a time.

13: sprinteur, puncheur, chanceur

For Stage 13 the weather relented. The grim, survival conditions of Stage 12 were replaced by thin, autumnal sunshine, and for a pleasant hundred-and-fifty-kilometre roll across the plains of the Po valley. The riders basked in this, in preparation for a punchy, forty-kilometre finale and the twin summits of the Roccolo and the Calaone.

This pair of climbs were clear puncheur territory. A handful of kilometres in length and with ramps up to eighteen, and twenty percent. Niche terrain for a very specific kind of rider. One who can attack, with ferocity, on a short, steep climb. A Diego Ulissi, perhaps? The Italian, Stage 2 winner and Giro d'Italia specialist (7 career stages to date) being the inform punchy climber in this race.

And we, the armchair fans, make our predictions. "Ok," we say, "I may lack the talent to win a hilly one-hundred-and-ninety-kilometre Giro stage but I have insight and knowledge. I understand what will happen." Which is code for I have watched an awful lot of bike racing on the telly, as the dent on my favourite spot on the couch will attest.

We had this all figured out. The punchy climbers have these two tough climbs during which to drop the sprinters. Any sprinters who can hang on will contest, and likely win, a sprint finish in the town of Monselice. The General Classification contenders will hover, attentive, but in defensive formation. They will leave the spoils to the punchy-climbing-fast-finishers and the sprinters-who-can-climb. Factoring in, of course, any plucky chancer (chanceur?) not quite fitting either mould but finding themselves on a good day and in a perky mood.

The Roccolo came first, and it did not disappoint. The pure sprinters, Elia Viviani and Arnaud Demare, were booted unceremoniously out the back. Peter Sagan held on. The two chased back just in time for the short, sharp ascent of the Calaone and a second shoe-ing. In fact, this time all three went pop to a greater (Demare and Viviani) or lesser (Sagan) extent.

From that summit it was sixteen kilometres to the finish. We had a thinned-out lead group of Ulissi-like fast finishers and General Classification men motivated for an on-the-rivet drive to the finish. Thirty seconds back were Sagan and fellow fast finisher Ben Swift (by name, and nature), who in turn were thirty seconds clear of Demare and Viviani.

And we're predicting again. If the Sagan group catches the led group then Sagan wins. If the Demare group catches the Sagan group which catches the lead group, then Demare wins. Viviani, whatever the scenario, doesn't win.

And what of these General Classification men in on the action; Almeida, in Pink, and young Tao Geoghegan-Hart (Ineos Grenadiers)? Both had climbed beautifully, with strength and control on the climbs, and now find themselves, by circumstance, dragged into the fight. They too now quite fancy a stage win and some bonus seconds.

Skinny climbers James Knox and Fausto Masnada, trusty lieutenants to Almeida, pulled the whole crew along in thrilling, near career-defining fashion. We got ahead of ourselves. "Whoop," we said, "if Almeida win this Giro THIS is a key moment!" Ignoring the many ifs and buts in that sentence in favour of raw edge-of-seat excitement.

Into town they rattled, the sprinters firmly at arm's length down the road, and a scruffy, ragtag sprint broke out. Almeida to the fore. He muscled, and bullied, and lurched for the line only for Diego Ulissi, with a desperate bike chuck, to snatch career Giro Stage win number eight from between the fingers of our Portuguese pal.

And with that comes tomorrows Stage 14 time-trial through Prosecco country. Maybe a glass of something fizzy if things go well, because from there on in we hit the tough terrain of the high mountains. Joao Almeida will be hoping Knox and Masnada didn't leave all their fight out on the road today.

Standings after Stage 13

Pink Jersey: Joao Almeida

2nd Wilko Kelderman (+56 seconds)

3rd Pello Bilbao (+2 minutes 11 seconds)

Cyclamen (sprint/points): Arnaud Demare

Blue (mountains): Ruben Guerreiro

Stages 14-15: Into the Dolomites

14: Almeida holds the cards

In a Grand Tour, the main contenders often finish on the same time on a given day. In a time-trial, no-one does. Like a shuffle of the deck deep into a massive game of snap, a TT is a bit of a faff but basically a good idea.

Our job today was to watch several dozen thin men ride through the Prosecco-producing vineyards of the Veneto, largely from behind. The qualities of their 'wiggle' our only guide as to their performance. Well, that and the clock; the race organisers choosing to use time to separate the riders today. Traditionalists.

It's a discipline that gives full reign to an often-well-hidden streak of nerdy obsession that runs through Eurosport's Bradley Wiggins; Wiggo having been the king of the TT in his pomp. When Brad is talking you through the dimples on the shoulders of skinsuit or the trick of Velcro-ing rear of helmet to neck-line of clothing as a reminder to keep your head up in the aero position, you remember that this is not the visceral thrill of a long-range attack in the mountains. This is high-speed stamp-collecting. It's insightful, and sort-of interesting, but it's not going to get the kids hashtagging is it?

What a TT does do, of course, is give us a good old look at the riders. They have nowhere to hide and we can watch them closely and pass judgement on their character, style and tiredness. And what we can say, without doubt, is that rarely has a rider looked so suited to a Pink Jersey (skinsuit) as Joao Almeida. He is the absolute incarnation of the calm, controlled, stylish, race-leading European pro cyclist. Immaculately turned-out. Unruffled. A deep, even Portuguese sun-tan and an unchanging expression that says: "how lovely of you to join me, chaps...it's always nice to have a group of fellow cyclists on hand to watch me win the bike race."

Is he really only twenty-two? Is this really his first Grand Tour? Can he really make it through week three, jersey intact, serene expression on his face?

Time will tell. In finishing sixth today Almeida extended his race lead to a minute over Wilko Kelderman, and more than two ahead of Pello Bilbao, surprise package Brandon McNulty (UAE Team Emirates), Vincenzo Nibali, and the rest. He was seemingly entirely unsurprised by the situation.

Beyond Almeida it was day for Filippo Ganna. Obviously. The near-unbeatable Italian TT specialist taking his third stage win of the race. Rohan Dennis got close, but the power produced through those huge Italian pistons is a sight to behold. More closely resembling a racehorse than a cyclist. Right now, throwing up a few fences and having a tiny person hit him with a whip might be the only way to stop him.

Much though they'll have enjoyed another Stage win Italy will, of course, be hoping Vincenzo Nibali can eat into Almeida's position in the final week and win the whole shebang. Slightly slower of leg these days, he will no doubt delve into his big bag 'o' tricks and attempt to prize Almeida away from Pink like the shell of a shucked oyster.

But in 2020, the year of the youngster, we're no longer surprised by near-adolescents winning bike races. For Almeida to win would be entirely in keeping. To have a man in his thirties as our victor would be a novelty.

Race Radio

What you Ganna do about it?

Team Ineos, following the abandonment of team leader and race favourite Geraint Thomas after his Stage 3 crash, had their hand forced. With the General Classification plan in tatters, they had a rethink. Removed from their Grand Tour controlling comfort zone there came a reinvention of the most unlikely kind: Ineos as free-spirited, opportunistic, breakaway specialists.

The team for whom the controlling of controllables represents their very reason for being found a new mission statement: to win stages, propel Tao Geoghegan-Hart as far up the rankings as possible, and have a jolly good time.

Chief protagonist in this regard has been Filippo Ganna. The prodigiously talented Italian track racer-cum-TT specialist bossed the opening time trial as expected, won a climber-friendly Stage 5 breakaway (causing social media to proclaim him the second coming of Spanish Tour legend Miguel Indurain in the process...calm down people!), clearly had the time of his life accompanying Peter Sagan part of the way along his Stage 10 masterpiece, and then won again, on the Stage 14 TT through Prosecco country.

In-between times, Ineos-wise, another breakaway stage was snaffled on Stage 12, to Cesenatico, by Jhonatan Narvaez.

To those of us who, while appreciating the unprecedented success of this British team had begun to tire of the relentless process management, it's an absolute joy to watch. Ganna – handsome, hugely stylish, prodigiously strong and apparently capable of doing whatever he likes on a bike - is the face of this new movement. Not so much marginal gains as huge, leaping gains, achieved with the minimum of planning and the handing over of day-to-day Grand Tour control to other, less exciting teams.

It's highly likely that this Giro is a one-off dictated by circumstance. That they'll revert back to grinding domination at the earliest opportunity. Which somehow makes this joyous aberration of a race all the more compelling.

15: Geoghegan-Hart plays the Pink piano

This was the moment. Joao Almeida, Grand Tour debutant and long-time Pink Jersey, faced the fight of his young life. On the steep ramps of the Piancavello Vincenzo Nibali dipped into his aforementioned bag and found it devoid of tricks. Cunning or otherwise. He was dropped. Fuglsang, Bilbao, McNulty, and anyone else with a dog in the fight was also long gone. And with seven kilometres to go the elastic snapped between our pristine Portuguese hero and a group of three who emerged at the head of the race: Wilko Kelderman, second place overall and threatening to rip Pink from Almeida's back, along with his teammate Jai Hindley (Team Sunweb) and London lad Tao Geoghegan-Hart.

Rob Hatch, on Eurosport, did that semi-growl he does to denote: "hey, viewer, something big's happening...LOOK!"

We looked. And we feared for Joao. On his twelfth day in Pink, the best-case mental maths we could manage had him losing it to Kelderman. We wondered what he was made of. Gasping and gaping in the late autumn sun he fought a ragged fight. Tongue lolling, all pretence of serenity gone, head tipped slightly back and twisting every ounce from every muscle, the boy was in pain.

Gapped by twenty, then thirty seconds, he held it. Critical but stable. Three against one and there are cracks, yes, but he wasn't cracking. Like a little Dutch lad with a thumb in a dyke he held back time to a trickle. He could, at any moment, lose minutes, but there were the leaders, always on the horizon, always in view. Radio long since ripped from his ear. The team car now silent. This was an internal battle.

Meanwhile, up the road, Tao Geoghegan-Hart was the boss. Sprightly, up on the pedals, catholic cross necklace in full swing, this felt like a coming of age. The twenty-five-year-old, having hovered around the top ten for much of the race, launched himself with a hail Mary and a "cheers Wilko...I'll be having the stage mate!" The moment he swung left on the finishing straight the win was his. Glorious!

Thirty-seven seconds later Almeida clawed his way to the finish, clinging to Pink by fifteen seconds. A HUGE ride of grit and character. Kelderman, having quietly negotiated fourteen stages without fanfare or mishap, clearly now his biggest challenger to win this Giro. Just to underline the enormous job done by his team Jai Hindley sits third overall. Geoghegan-Hart is fourth.

All of which epic drama had seemed a world away eighty-odd kilometres previously, as the peloton had ridden whimsically past a piano festooned with Pink balloons furiously banging out some mid-stage tunes. The fifteen-year-old boy in me chuckling away at the idea of someone playing the pink piano in public. As euphemisms go, almost certainly illegal.

I'd wager that everyone in this race is very happy indeed with the prospect of a rest-day. The cynic in me wonders if Nibali's capitulation paves the way for the Italian race-organisers to bow to Covid-pressure and halt the race early. The realist in me thinks that with only six stage to go it's Millan or bust. The romantic in me is too busy revelling in a fantastic bike race to get bogged down in all of that.

Standings after Stage 15

Pink Jersey: Joao Almeida

2nd Wilko Kelderman (+15 seconds)

3rd Jai Hindley (+2 minutes 56 seconds)

Cyclamen (sprint/points): Arnaud Demare

Blue (mountains): Giovanni Visconti

Stages 16-18: Mountains...BIG ones!

16: brawn, brain, and a breakaway win

Half-way up the final climb of the day and Aussie Ben O'Connor (NTT Pro Cycling) made his move. Casting thoughts of a resigned roll to the line from his mind he chose to inflict pain upon himself. Deserting his companions, digging deep, exploring the depths of his lungs in search of stage leader Jan Tratnik (Bahrain-McLaren).

And it was third time lucky. Our circuit in and around the town of San Daniele del Friuli taking us three times up the slopes of the Monte di Ragogna. Just shy of three kilometres, averaging nearly eleven percent, designed, cunningly, to hurt cyclists who attack. Tratnik, in the lead, measuring his effort while chaser O'Connor bust a gut.

By the summit the catch was made; but what damage had O'Connor done?

Vuelta Espana alert!

It's been a weird year. And just when we thought we'd seen it all we get overlapping Grand Tours. A Giro d'Italia and a Vuelta Espana, running in parallel, in October.

What unhinged madness is this?

While Joao Alemida carried the Pink jersey serenely through Stage 16 in Friuli it was kicking off over in the Basque Country.

In order to preserve your sanity, dear reader, that race will follow this one in a few pages time. I will not summarise them concurrently.

But know this: in documenting 'the great overlap' my mental bandwidth was stretched, at times, paper thin.

Now...where were we?

Fifteen minutes back and the peloton were cruising. The decision made two hundred kilometres ago that the break would have its day. Deceuninck Quickstep sat visible on the front in service of their man, Almeida, in Pink. 'An easy day,' we, the viewing public pronounce, dismissively glossing over the distance and the four thousand metres of vertical ascent of this sixteenth stage.

Tratnik had launched on episode two of our three-part Ragogna mini-series. The break broke into three; our leader, a motivated chase group (British champ Ben Swift to the fore), and a final group of (by now) hand waving, head-shaking, former companions turned grumpy rivals. Mutinous. Finger-pointing for the cameras as the win rode off down the road.

Into town came Tratnik and O'Connor, and the Slovenian - and I apologise in advance for the technical terminology - did him up like an absolute kipper. With a kilometre-and-a-half to go Tratnik calculated that the gap back to the chasers was unassailable. They would not be caught. He could afford to locate O'Connor's rear wheel and firmly glue himself there.

On the final steep ramp, the lanky climber had no choice. From the front, he gave it the beans for two hundred metres. All or nothing. Now or never.

Nothing.

Never.

His legs piped up: remember that effort back on the Ragogna? Well, we're done mate. Tratnik, with impeccable timing, summoned all the energy he'd saved and dispatched him. To the line. Grand Tour career stage win number one, just two hours down the road from his Slovenian home town of Ljubljana. Brawn, brain, and breakaway win.

17: full-gas-crying

We met Ben O'Connor, the bean-pole Aussie climber, yesterday. This guy really wants to be a pro cyclist. The main sponsor of his team, NTT, are throwing the towel in at the end of this season, and O'Connor has set up camp in the shop window and is going nowhere until someone snaps him up. Yesterday he bust a gut for the privilege of a breakaway defeat to Slovenian Jan Tratnik. Today, Stage 17, he was back for more.

From within the lead group, on this massive day of late-Giro mountains, he launched his marketing campaign on the lower slopes of the Madonna de Campiglio, site of our summit finish. With one, big kick, he was gone. Solidly in form, pushing powerfully through the pedals, he would not be caught. A win by force of will. A great advert (as with Alex Dowsett, back on Stage 8) for the motivational powers of pending unemployment.

Post-stage, on reflection, he explained he had been 'full-gas-crying' after the win. Possibly the most pro cyclist description of emotion it's possible to give (super-weepy coming a close second). He has certainly done all he can to tempt any potential sponsors out there to part with their money.

Back down the road, the peloton was in full trundle. With Covid restrictions and possible snow threatening to disrupt the coming days, this stage had to be the day. Pink Jersey Joao Almeida had to be attacked, de-robed, and sent a-tumbling down the rankings. Because time is running out. The clock is ticking. And so, while O'Connor and his pals did their thing up front, we watched the General Classification contenders and we waited.

And waited.

And then we got a coffee and some snacks. Some of us had a little nap. We flicked around the channels. We made whimsical anagrams out of Team NTT's Amanuel Ghebreigzabhier and we waited some more. The peloton crossed the Forcella Valbona and the Monte Bondone. Crested the Passo Durone. Almeida's team on the front, keeping it steady, had it all under control. Onto the Campiglio. A couple of test-yer-legs moves from

Sunweb and Ineos, and Almeida sat tight. And remained tight, to the summit, where the contenders finished largely intact.

Truth be told, not the fireworks we might have hoped for.

Tomorrow, Stage 18, weather permitting, is the mighty, legendary, Passo dello Stelvio. Stuff will happen. You have my word. Though maybe don't expect Ben O'Connor to be up front again. He has every right to be full-gas-tired.

18: high drama on the Stelvio

"Just how good is Joao Almeida," we've been wondering, "and can he actually go on and win the thing?!" Alas no. After fifteen stages in pink the sixteenth was too much. It featured the mighty Passo dello Stelvio, see. Twenty-five kilometres of steep Tarmac and uncountable hairpin bends. Half way up this great mountain, the air thinning, our Portuguese prodigy cracked. Suffering, tiny against the immense backdrop, and sliding backwards, he was in damage limitation mode many miles from the summit.

And the Stelvio is no respecter of reputation. As an increasingly small group clung to their faculties Fuglsang, Nibali, Pozzovivo —ninety-five percent of the peloton, in fact - suffered the same fate.

Just four would scrabble to the to contest the mountain, the stage, and the race: teammates Tao Geoghegan-Hart and Rohan Dennis from Ineos, and Wilko Kelderman and Jai Hindley from Sunweb. The fight for pink had taken on a new shape.

Next to falter was Kelderman. Attached, limpet-like to his teammate's wheel one minute, edged gently off, and away like Leo DiCaprio, off the bow of the Titanic and into the depths of the North Atlantic the next. Hindley in the Kate Winslet role. Heartbroken. One lingering look and he's gone.

Over the summit (and after an absurdly tense battle between Jai Hindley and the zip of his jacket – seriously, YouTube it!), the three swooped down into the next valley from where time trial specialist Rohan Dennis got to work. He pulled the two youngsters across to the base of the final climb before waving them off, "have fun kids," for a final ten-kilometre climb to the finish. One final shuffle of this haphazard deck of a peloton, scattered chaotically down the road. These two, and not discounting the gritty Kelderman a minute behind, on the brink of contesting the outcome of the entire Giro d'Italia, right here, right now.

Hindley, team leader Kelderman behind him, had a ready-made excuse to sit on Geoghegan-Hart's wheel with a "who, me...well I can't attack my leader can I Tao?" The Londoner was compelled to do the hard graft. And so up the climb he pulled them towards the beauty spot of Laghi di Cancano. Others were chasing bravely back after the decimation of the Stelvio – Jakob Fuglsang and Pello Bilbao to the fore – but our leaders were clear. The final hairpins, a rise to the line, and Hindley snuck out from Geoghegan-Hart's wheel for a stage win. Cruel on the Brit, calculating by the Aussie.

And we count back.

Riders begin to land.

Kelderman, two minutes eighteen seconds back, snatches the Pink Jersey. He sits twelve seconds clear of Jai Hindley who is three more ahead of Tao Geoghegan-Hart. Three-thousand-kilometres and a single, well placed Stelvio, and the top three are separated by fifteen seconds. FIFTEEN!

Spare a thought for João Almeida, but we have an ALMIGHTY bike race on our hands.

Standings after Stage 18

Pink Jersey: Wilko Kelderman

2nd Jai Hindley (+12 seconds)

3rd Tao Geoghegan-Hart (+15 seconds)

Cyclamen (sprint/points): Arnaud Demare

Blue (mountains): Ruben Guerreiro

Stages 19-21: A Rebel Alliance and a Grand Finale

19: solidarity

With ten kilometres to go a chasing group of five are riding through-and-off like clockwork. Working together, sharing the effort, it was a lesson in smooth solidarity between riders with a shared goal: to catch Czech rider Josef Cerny (Team CCC). The lone leader thirty seconds down the road through the late season gloom on the road to Asti.

Our finish town being a prestige place in Italian wine. Whether you fancy a sparkling white (Asti Spumanti) or a premium Red (Barbera) you could do worse than head here. Cerny, a man on a mission, in search of a tipple.

And talking of solidarity the entire peloton chose today, Stage 19, to band together, brother-in-arms, in a show of defiance. After the mammoth mountains of recent days today was to be the longest Stage of the race (258 kilometres), a pan-flat schlepp through wind and rain.

"Enough," said the riders, as one.

A start-line protest, a rider rebellion, a team bus transfer knocking more than a hundred kilometres off the route, and threats from Giro boss Mauro Vegni of lawyers and repercussions. "Someone will pay," he said, menacingly, presumably while shaking a comic-book fist in the direction of Adam Hansen, rider representative on the cyclists Union the CPA.

The result: the longest stage became the shortest. "We will race one-hundred-and-twenty-four kilometres...no more" declared the peloton, in unison.

And they did.

Lunga vita alla rivoluzione!

None of which explains how Cerny stayed away for the win. We have a rudimentary understanding of human physiology and the laws of physics. Five riders sharing the load are quicker than one. No matter how determined.

And yet. Let's walk it through. The gap is dropping, but slowly...so slowly. The five leaders are giving concerted, co-ordinated chase, to tiny effect. Could it be – perish the thought – that some of those five are affecting the appearance of full-gas while delivering, what, four-fifths gas? Three quarters gas?

Five kilometres to go and the gap is twenty seconds. Three kilometres to go and it's seventeen.

Let's name the five: Simon Clarke (EF Pro Cycling), Sander Armee (Lotto-Soudal), Victor Campanaerts, Jacopo Mosca (Trek-Segafredo), Iljo Keisse (Deceuninck-Quickstep). Somebody, somewhere, is saving their legs. Assuming the catch and planning the sprint. Undermining the cohesion of the group.

With a kilometre to go Cerny is clear. Through town, a twenty second gap back to the chase, and it's hand over mouth for a "oh-my-God-I've-won" finish line salute. A hail-Mary burst from Campanaerts proving too little, too late. Cerny wins. Solidarity wins. The peloton, ten minutes down the road, enjoying a nice day off, also wins.

20: On a knife-edge

Stage 20 was to be a huge, epic, mountainous trek across the Colle dell' Agnello, Col d'Izoard, and the Col de Montgenèvre, on the way to the ski-resort of Sestriere. Huge in stature, it would loom over even Stage 18 as the defining set-piece of this year's race. Alas, as so often this year, Covid-19 intervened. The French authorities, not allowing passage across their borders, put paid to all that.

But we mustn't complain. Mid-race, way back on the Adriatic coast, the entire enterprise had hung in the balance. At one point, the noises coming from the race suggested that the prospect of a full three-week race reaching completion was fanciful. It just wasn't going to happen. That we have reached Stage 20, and will finish tomorrow in Milan, is a win.

For our Stage 20 reboot we had our planned start in Alba and swapped our multi-col extravaganza for three ascents up to Sestriere; once up the main road, and then twice in through the steeper, windier back way. Best of all, the whole damn race was up for grabs. Our top three – Kelderman, Hindley and Geoghegan-Hart – separated by a miniscule fifteen seconds.

Setting the pace at the front of a tired, thinning peloton, was Rohan Dennis; Geoghegan-Hart's teammate taking on mountain domestique duties with complete relish. Second time up the climb it was simply too much for Kelderman. The race leader (and Hindley's teammate and leader, don't forget) was simply ridden out of contention. His Giro has been a slow-burning, near-three-week vigil of staying in contention and never putting a foot wrong. Never setting the race alight but positioning himself to take advantage as others slipped away. And now, on Stage 20, at the hands of a TT specialist Dennis, he was reduced cruelly to rubble. He would end the day in third overall. His lieutenant Jai Hindley apparently born ready to assume the team leadership mantle.

But Dennis was not done. Looping down off the mountain and back around for ascent number three he was still there. On the front. Setting the pace as the third man in a two-way battle between Hindley and Geoghegan-Hart. This, with the rest of the peloton reduced to bit-part players, would set up tomorrow's final day time trial and our Giro d'Italia winner.

Into the final three kilometres we waited for an attack. We wondered who had the legs and who was hanging on. Hindley, unable to hold back no longer, struck. Geoghegan-Hart was immediately right, and I mean RIGHT, on his wheel, overlapping for effect. Hindley slowed. Dennis came back, basically un-droppable. Hindley repeated the move. This went on for a while. Attack, follow, slow, attack, follow, slow. No-one giving a millimetre. Hindley throwing his kitchen sink and a whole cupboard full of pots, pans and utensils at his new nemesis. Geoghegan-Hart, barely buckling, would not crack.

Into the final kilometre and our two were side by side, shoulder to shoulder and literally touching at times. Separated by four seconds on the General Classification. The race could only be closer had Geoghegan-Hart leapt across onto Hindley's back and ridden him to the finish line. He didn't.

Instead, with one move – his single attack of the day – Geoghegan-Hart picked his moment to swept around his rival and take a glorious sprint to the line. The bonus seconds ensuring that after twenty stages of mountains, sprints, weather, and drama, the pair of them are dead level. The race organisers, consulting some kind of hidden football-style VAR system, putting Hindley in Pink. From Geoghegan-Hart it was back slaps all-round for Rohan Dennis, who pulled the whole thing along to place these two gladiators, by hand, up onto this knife-edged pedestal, and etch his own name into Giro folklore.

Tomorrow, Stage 21, we have a fifteen-kilometre time-trial in Milan. Whoever of these two rides faster over fifteen kilometres is the new winner of the Giro d'Italia. Simple as that.

21: Tao Geoghegan-Hart...Giro winner!

Sir Bradley Wiggins was rambling and emotional in the Eurosport commentary box. Sir Dave Brailsford, team boss at Ineos, was cuddling anyone at the finish line (and within the Covid-secure bubble, of course) who moved. Knights of the Realm everywhere forgoing calm rationality in favour of the sheer humanity of the situation. Rob Hatch, the voice of cycling, had gone up a couple of octaves.

All of which told us that Tao Geoghegan-Hart – London lad, top notch cyclist, and all-round cheeky monkey – had only gone and actual won the actual Giro d'Italia. We can only imagine the celebrations back home in Hackney, East London. Some old dear knockin' out a tune on the ol' Joanna, cockles and whelks all-round: "Well blow me dahn wiv a fever and crack open the bubbly, we're 'avin a Moriarty."

Having begun the day level on time with Jai Hindley – the first time this has ever happened in the history of Grand Tour cycling – fifteen kilometres of city centre time-trialling would give us a winner. At least we hoped it would. Because finishing level again, after this, would lead to all kinds of count-back shenanigans and give a us a winner with a horribly unsatisfactory taste in our mouths.

The tension, as it turned out, was yesterday, when our man had responded to the repeated attacks of Hindley. Today, from the moment he'd safely negotiated the start ramp the pressure was released. Out on the course, a flat, straight, fifteen kilometres into the heart of Milan, it became simple. Pushing efficiently through the pedals, a highly refined aero position to the fore, the Giro belonged to Tao.

From our first time-check we could see it. From there, with no climbs, few corners, and limited opportunity to exploit a weakness and claw back a deficit, Hindley would not challenge him. It was the truest 'race of truth' ever seen.

Geoghegan-Hart's teammate Filippo Ganna had mullered the

course earlier in the day to guarantee an Ineos Stage win. Now our little cockney sparrow, the calmest man in Europe, was trampling all over his spirited rival; the fact that Hindley would wear Pink, on the road in this Giro, for a mere eighteen minutes in total, was usurped only by the even quirkier fact that Geoghegan heart would slip into it for the first and only time on the Milanese podium.

We've watched him morph before our eyes from loyal lieutenant, to free-spirited attacker, to crisp, calm, Giro contender, and win one of the closest Grand Tours in history. In a year of curveballs and random events, Tao Geoghegan-Hart winning the Giro d'Italia is amongst the curviest, most random, and downright entertaining of them all.

Giro d'Italia Final Standings

Pink Jersey: Tao Geoghegan-Hart

2nd Jai Hindley (+39 seconds)

3rd Wilko Kelderman (+1 minute 29 seconds)

Cyclamen(sprint/points): Arnaud Demare

Blue(mountains): Ruben Guerreiro

Our new Giro winner has a much sought-after talent; a God-given ability to recover, and endure, and maintain his form and fitness deep into a three-week race. We've seen this before. He was attacking and visible at the thick end of the 2019 Vuelta Espana, as others fell away and faltered, to finish an on-the-up twentieth overall. Here at the Giro, we saw a supercharged version of this.

He'd announced himself on Stage 13. A flat stage punctuated by a couple of punchy climbs saw the General Classification riders at the head of the race and testing their legs. And there was Tao. Calmly climbing with that elegant, upright style. Catholic cross swaying around his neck. Still down in twelfth position overall, two minutes fifty-five behind race leader Joao Almeida, and not really on our collective radar, but showing quiet signs of form.

With his win on Stage 15, where the first cracks in Almeida's resolve began to appear, he announced this fact through the great megaphone of a late-Grand-Tour-summit-finish-win at Piancavello. As the accumulated effects of fatigue began to bite he took the first Grand Tour stage win of his career, ending that day sitting fourth overall, and it was officially ON! From there, he was faultless. Un-droppable.

Back at the Tour de France, Tadej Pogacar had been a surprise winner, but more in the manner of the win than the fact of it. The young Slovenian had widely been considered a young contender. A dark horse. A maybe. Tao Geoghegan-Hart, on the other hand, talented and sprightly though he is, was no-one's pick to win the Giro. This was leftfield.

And for his team - the Ineos Grenadiers - the race was a triumph. With the abandonment of team leader Geraint Thomas, we saw a recalibration of objectives, and a joyous and carefree incarnation of this usually buttoned-down team. They backed up the overall win with a seven-stage haul from future (if not current) megastar of the sport Filippo Ganna (four), Jhonatan Narvaez (one), and Geoghegan-Hart (two).

The virus, of course, had always bubbled away in the background to complicate matters. As the race traversed Emilia Romagna mid-race, reports of rising Italian Covid cases had cross-referenced with the sight of fans out on the road and the nervous mutterings of teams and riders. The end had felt nigh. One might still argue against the wisdom of a massive bike race criss-crossing a country in the midst of a pandemic. But they found a way. Yet one more exuberant instalment to add to the Giro d'Italia roll of honour.

Vuelta Espana

I'm (admittedly quite grandly) calling this The Great Overlap. The Vuelta Espana has begun and yes, equally, your eyes do not deceive you, the Giro d'Italia is still on. Normally separated by months, these races find themselves plonked atop one another and forced to run concurrently and make do. This doesn't feel healthy.

It's long been said (by the keepers of cycling folklore) that to ride a Grand Tour shortens a cyclist's life. That the sheer dig-deep extremity of the undertaking makes you die. While the same is not quite true for the TV fan, spectating on a Grand Tour - each stage, every day, for three weeks – is no small feat. Like reading a long, dense, richly rewarding but mentally taxing novel.

Imagine ploughing through The Name of the Rose in one hand whilst digesting The Sun Also Rises in the other. Before long your fourteenth century Franciscan monks have given up their Italian abbey and are bullfighting, knocking back cocktails, and musing on life and love, Hemingway-style, in the bars of Pamplona. Not un-entertaining, perhaps, but confusing, difficult to chronologise, and likely to induce headaches in reader and writer alike.

So, while Belgian puncheur Tim Wellens is quietly winning in a sleepy Galician village perched atop a fearsome Spanish hill, Tao Geoghegan-Hart and Jai Hindley are self-harming at high altitude while experts argue about the difference between a Dolomite and an Alp over a mid-afternoon espresso. It's dissonant, confusing, and kind of exhilarating. Like many aspects of 2020 it's not a thing I would like to repeat, but I'm embracing the lunatic oddness as best I can.

It's also worth noting that this Vuelta, in this time-crunched calendar, has shortened to eighteen stages from the regular twenty-one. The race will largely steer clear of the mountainous south, the Mediterranean coast, and the lizard hot central regions in favour of the lush, green, autonomous areas of the north. Expect late-season weather, Atlantic Ocean views, leg-breakingly steep climbs through damp air, and an awful lot of x's and t's in the place names.

After wins for Pogacar and Geoghegan-Hart so far this year, it would take a total fool to make a prediction on a Vuelta winner. Well, okay then...it's between Primoz Roglic and Richard Carapaz for the Red Jersey but don't, whatever you do, rule out some physically freakish twenty-year-old appearing, unannounced, to sweep up all the jerseys, several stages, and the hearts of an adoring cycling public in the process.

Stages 1-3: Full Pelt, No Holds Barred

1: the man with three lungs

The Giro d'Italia is ongoing, and exciting. Which means the Vuelta must do something to grab our attention. So why not kick it off with one of those mucky, windswept Basque Country days? A profile of dark, steep climbs, falling leaves blowing hither and thither across the Tarmac, and a frankly insane pace.

The riders clearly got a memo this morning: "look, lads, everyone is watching the Giro, we need something special today to divert those eyeballs in our direction. Also, what with Covid 'n' all that, this Vuelta will last about three days, four at best...forget about the long game, just get out there and RACE!"

The early stages, in any normal year, of any normal Grand Tour, are not the time for eventual winners to show their cards. With an eye on the challenges to come they sit tight, stay safe, and let other, more opportunistic types take centre stage. But what is normal anymore? It's Stage 1 and the big names are riding like an early race leading Red Jersey might not be an altogether bad idea. Because if Covid kicks in, the race gets abandoned, and the organiser are looking for a way to award a winner, there's surely no harm in finding yourself in Red. Nudge, nudge, wink, wink...

On the day's penultimate climb, the Ineos Grenadiers are DRILLING it! Chris Froome, on the comeback from injury, is lolling and hanging off the back of a still seventy-strong peloton. The cameras pan back for a look, intruding on his struggles. The Ineos leader in spirit but not, alas, in form, showing immediately that he is a long way from Grand Tour contention. His teammates push on, accepting him as collateral damage. Richard Carapaz (Ineos Grenadiers), Giro d'Italia winner of 2019, the confirmed team leader a mere two-thirds into Stage 1.

Onto the final climb, the Alto de Arrete - five kilometres of ramps and sheer drops - and Ineos are still going on the front. And then, BANG! Sepp Kuss (Team Jumbo-Visma), the American - the Man With Three Lungs - nails it. Accelerating away in a move to drop teammate Tom Dumoulin (Team Jumbo-Visma), Spanish veteran Alejandro Valverde (Movistar Team), and a whole cadre of fine bike riders. This breathless stage sharpened to a fine point. Into the closing kilometres and we are down to eight for a sleeves-rolled-up General Classification battle on day one.

There's Dan Martin (Israel Start-up Nation) looking sprightly (in that downtrodden, nodding style); Esteban Chaves (Mitchelton-Scott) smiling away, as ever; Primoz Roglic (Team Jumbo-Visma), hovering, like a man with an iron strong teammate (Kuss) and a simmering memory of Tour de France disaster; and Hugh Carthy (EF Pro Cycling): tall, pink, northern, and unable to resist any longer.

Bosh! Carthy attacks. Two kilometres to go. The summit is crested and a fast, windy finish awaits. The chasers chase, the TV camera bike on their tale, and we all, as one, remember we can breathe if we want. There are seventeen stages still remaining and the Vuelta Espana is full-gas ON!

And then off darts Primoz Roglic. One burst of cathartic, Tour de France losing aggression, and that's that. Like a powerful rat up a picturesque Basque drainpipe to win and cap, as opening Grand Tour stages go, a modern classic.

2: shits-and-giggles

Are we sure this is a Grand Tour? Can someone check? Where is the caginess and the calculation? Why is no-one, after two stages, even pretending to try and save energy? It's fantastic, and I can't wait to see what happens when they all run out of puff in a few days. Yesterday, Stage 1, we had a bonkers cat-and-mouse devil-may-care GC-battle to the finish line. Today, our set piece climb to the Alto de San Miguel de Aralar and descent off the other side into Lekunberri promised similar, but had a twist.

The start town of Pamplona, see, is the home of Spain's team, Movistar. Home roads. High expectations. Pressure, in a poor season to date, to perform. And to their credit they didn't shirk. They controlled, and bossed, and used their numbers. On the climb of the San Miguel they cranked up the pace and made it hard. Heading to the summit, on your standards issue battle-scarred Spanish concrete road surface, the peloton was decimated. Reduced to a dozen. As per Stage 1, General Classification men almost to a man.

Cresting the summit, and faced with several kilometres of sinuous descent, Movistar sent perennial naughty schoolboy and team mascot Marc Soler (Movistar Team) off the front and on the attack. If you watched the Netflix series "The Least Expected Day" recently, which charted the travails of the team through 2019, you'll know Soler as the fresh-faced young buck with the "what...me?" face and the air of insubordinate mischief. The team had talked of him being a leader in 2020. This was his moment.

Having clearly memorised every kink and bend for this very moment he was immediately twenty seconds clear, and then he was gone; out of reach of the chasers, always hidden around the next bend, local knowledge to the fore. He could not be caught. Winning his first Vuelta Stage in delighted style he revelled, at the finish, in the approval of old man Alejandro Valverde – teammate and elder-statesman. Soler, if he didn't quite start the race a boy and finish it a man, certainly climbed a rung on the ladder.

Behind him...yep, another cat-and-mouse devil-may-care General Classification battle for bonus seconds, kudos, and general shits and giggles. As per. Roglic won the sprint, with Dan Martin, Hugh Carthy, Richard Carapaz, Esteban Chaves, Sepp Kuss, et al, close behind. Are there even any domestiques in the race? If there are, send 'em home. We'll just watch team leaders race for two-and-a-half weeks.

3: the horrible effectiveness of Dan Martin

Dan Martin is a fine, race-winning pro cyclist. But he is not a pretty sight in full flight. His is not the liquid pedal stroke of a Richard Carapaz or the stock-still serenity of Primoz Roglic. He is frenzy. In early effort he nods, and wrangles, and bends the bike to his will. In deep, ragged attack he is twisted and gnarly. Rictus faced and jerk-bodied.

This, Stage 3, was a rugged schlepp through **Castile and León**; geographically the largest autonomous community in Spain. Broken up by a pair of categorized climbs it was uphill almost from flag to line. A four man break in the clear, a peloton in hot pursuit, and an eight-kilometre climb to a summit finish at Laguna Negra. Need I say, the General Classification contenders were up for another scrap.

The run-in to the climb was a narrow, forested affair. Wet roads, clouds hanging low, the dank waft of moss and bark palpable through our TV screens. The peloton caught the break at the base and we knew what would come.

The big teams – Ineos, Jumbo-Visma - would come to the fore and ratchet up the pace. As the climb steepened towards the summit the field would whittle and wane in size. Sepp Kuss would be visible, the strongest man in the world, taking one breath to everyone else's two. In the final two kilometres the sniping attacks would come. Random riders – a Kenny Elissonde (Trek-Segafredo) here, a Clement Champoussin (AG2R La Mondiale) there – making bold moves before dying gloriously. In the end, as is the wont of this crazy Vuelta, we would be left with our cast of big names.

Vlasov (Astana), Mas (Movistar Team), Grosschartner (Bora-Hansgrohe) and Carthy hovered, and hung in, before Dan Martin unleashed himself. Timing his move from two hundred metres out, like a starved animal catching a sniff of raw meat, he launched down the left; a move of horrible effectiveness. The Green points jersey across his back, clashing horribly with the blue of his Israel Start-up Nation kit to juice up the visual violence, he dug and scrabbled his way to the line to win, gloriously, from Red Jersey Roglic and Polka Dotted Carapaz.

A huge win. He talked of his family, and a tough year, and the emotional resonance of the moment. There were tears and humanity, a big-hearted warmth, and then an apology. For allowing weakness to seep from his eyes in the form of tears. Such is the buttoned-down lot of the high performing pro sportsman.

Standings after Stage 3

Red Jersey: Primoz Roglic

2nd Dan Martin (+5 seconds)

3rd Richard Carapaz (13 seconds)

Green (sprint/points): Primoz Roglic

Polka dots (mountains): Richard Carapaz

Long Shadows

This Vuelta Espana looks different. And not just because everyone is masked up and the roadside is bereft of fans. The late season pre-winter slant of the sunshine gives the whole show a different complexion. Brown leaves leap from the trees and flutter across our screens, betwixt and between the massed ranks of the peloton, to gather roadside.

We've got more rain, mist, darkness and drizzle than your average Vuelta. Gone are the standard issue forty-degree days through parched landscape to be replaced by something a little more seasonal. Technical clothing is being worn – rain capes, knee-warmers, and overshoes – and the sun-cream manufacturers are having a lean year.

It's still demonstrably a Vuelta Espana. The racing is harem-scarem and the peloton is packed with riders of mixed late-season motivation. The climbs are still masochistic and steep. But the weather is northern European.

As we know, and in the words of ex-pro and now TV expert David Millar, the Vuelta is a "hot bastard." This is what it does. Therein lies the challenge and appeal. There's a certain novelty value to a chilly, nippy,

159

windswept Vuelta, but let's get back to normal next year, shall we?

Stages 4-6: The North-East

4: Sam Bennett is on the black stuff

The last time we saw Sam Bennett (Deceuninck-Quickstep) was on the Champs Elysees. Green bike raised above his green head he had just won the concluding sprint of the Tour de France to claim the Green Jersey. As moments go that's tough to beat. Career defining. Should he never win another bike race he could retire a success. We would certainly have forgiven him following up that achievement with a few weeks of drinking Guinness and enjoying the craic. Easing off and piling a few pounds on. Based on today, he's done nothing of the sort.

After three stages of chaotic disruption, day four at the Vuelta gave us something more standard. The stage to Numancia, though lumpy and bumpy in places, was as flat as you'll get in this race. Your classic four-man breakaway group was given a regulation four-minute lead. The race then rumbled through the countryside for a couple of hours, in control, a sprint finish on everyone's mind.

Sure, we enjoyed watching the two BH-Burgos riders carry out their contractual obligation to "be on the telly as much as possible": Willie Smit and Jesus Ezquerrra (both BH Burgos) from the small Spanish team doing a stirling job as doomed cannon fodder. Smit, in particularly, gurned spectacularly and gave it the full "ahh, man, I'm so disappointed" upon the catch, as Numancia appeared on the horizon. Doing his best to maintain the pretence of a possible stage win.

Break caught, and still several kilometres from the finish, the helicopter camera panned out to show us a wide, arrow-straight road into town. A tailwind on their backs, the peloton scorched along at sixty-kilometres an hour; too fast for even the most-foolhardy to attempt a late guerrilla lurch for the line. Today, as sure as eggs are eggs, was a sprint finish.

Ok Sam, cards on table. How're the legs? Just how lairy did the post-Tour celebrations get?

Into town, screaming along at seventy K's an hour, Bennett's Quickstep crew were firmly on the front. One-by-one and in total control. Poised to deliver their man to open up his gigantic sprint and sledgehammer the opposition. But Team UAE had a plan. Banking on Bennett having partied post-Tour they launched Jasper Philipsen (UAE Team Emirates), BOOM!, like a peak-era Michael Johnson off the final bend in the four hundred metres...and gone. Seven, eight metres clear, in a blink.

Bennett, like a Dublin barfly at the call of last orders, sparked into to life. A big step on the gas, a huge delivery of power, and the gap is down to five, three, one...still accelerating, he crosses the line to win from MILES back. WOW! A statement. An affirmation from Bennett of his Alpha status.

It's long been a thing in Ireland to drink Guinness, for health.

Packed full of iron, swirling with mystical, life-giving powers. At the risk of perpetuating a national stereotype could the black stuff be the secret to Sam Bennett's success? Good things come to those who wait, as they say.

5: where there's a Wellens there's a way

It's a niche area of interest, admittedly, but I could happily spend an afternoon watching Tim Wellens (Lotto-Soudal) ride his bike. Ideally from side-on. With that flat backed, long-limbed style, and a fluid pedal stroke, he is a picture of powerful efficiency.

I count myself fortunate to feel this way. In these times of overlapping Grand Tours, and having leapt up and down in front of the telly earlier in the day at the sight of Tao Geoghegan-Hart, in the Giro d'Italia, as he arm-wrestled Jai Hindley to the summit at Sestriere, Stage 5 of the Vuelta was going to have to come up with something awfully diverting to compete.

Tim Wellens in the breakaway, while not offering the tension and high-stakes excitement of the Giro, was enough. On a hilly, if not mountainous day, up in north-eastern Spain and on the fringes of the Pyrenees, the peloton took a relative easy day. Themselves content, perhaps, to imagine the sight of Wellens, stylish, and away up the road, to help them pass the kilometres.

Cresting the final climb with fifteen to go our three leaders had a fast glide towards the town of Sabinanigo and a steep ramp of a finish to the line. Wellens found himself in the company of Guillaume Martin

(Cofidis) and young Dutchman Thyman Arensman (Tea Sunweb). Martin, the likeable and professorial French climber and Arensman...well, pphhfffshht...who knows!? I suppose this is yet another precocious youngster I need to learn about in this year of precocious youngsters. I am seriously starting to wonder whether processing all these new cyclists is pushing older, useful information out of my brain to make space. I could've sworn I used to be able to speak French, for example, but now: Sacre bleu! Je ne suis plus si sûr.

So. Wellens will be strong, and wily, and will power up that final climb like the thoroughbred classics man that he is. Martin will give it a good old go but will probably fall short on account of the climb being puncheur rather than grimpeur territory (hmm, maybe the French vocab is still there after all!?). Which leaves Arensman to do whatever his thing is. Go on, 2020...surprise me. He's going to attack from three kilometres out, ride the climb no-handed, and win the stage by a minute, right?

Wrong.

Wellens distracted the pair of them through town with his silky style before outlasting them on the climb for a muscular win. Reassuring, in a way, that sometimes the tried and trusted, time-honoured wisdom we gather about our favourite cyclists turns out to be true. These are stages that Tim Wellens wins, and he does it exactly like that. Thyman Arensman: your time will probably come. Let us enjoy the older guys for a while first, eh?

As for the peloton? Primoz Roglic muscled his way up that finishing slope in what could only be viewed as a visible, dominant message to everyone else in the race that: "I am the strongest, I'm also still pissed off about the Tour, and there's not really much point in you all being here, to be honest."

We will see.

Because we've been here before haven't we, Primoz me ol' mate?

6: Hugh Carthy, amid the cloud and the chaos

Peering through the gloom it was possible to make out some cyclists. Groups of them, in dribs and drabs, surviving their way up the Formigal; this Pyrenean ski-resort, our finish for Stage 6. The weather, in a word, was grim. Like Flanders, at altitude, in October. Cloud hanging down low, rain-obscured TV cameras, and team colours disguised beneath rain jackets made rider ID a simple guessing game.

Roglic there, I think? Pretty sure that's Esteban Chaves? Is that, wait...Miguel Indurain!?

It wasn't.

One man, thankfully, more visible that the rest, was Hugh Carthy; six feet four, head to toe in pink (because, to HELL with rain jackets!), and fully committed to dropping a massive wet grenade onto Primoz Roglic and his pals.

With remnants of the breakaway dropping back, and other riders on the attack, every-man-for-himself, scattered along every yard of this bleak climb, Carthy saw his moment. With Roglic struggling he and Richard Carapaz (probably...tough to say!?) gritted their teeth and seized the day. The Ecuadorian, a mountain man from a tough training climate and Carthy, from the North-West of England (aka the wettest place in the world), better equipped than most in these conditions.

For we viewers, to even sit and watch on the telly for too long was to risk compromising our immune systems. But our daring duo were unfazed. Hence why we are sitting watching and eating cake and they are busy being the stuff of legend.

Towards the finish, Basque rider Ion Izaguirre (Astana) was away and hanging on for a breakaway win. Then came a group of chasers. And then, marvellously, came Carthy. Those rake thin legs levering his bike one way and t'other in fine, pink style. Having been up the front at every crucial occasion so far in this Vuelta he now sits a rather exciting second overall.

Following Carthy came Carapaz, seven seconds back. The Ecuadorian (and now former, with the recent glorious ascent of Tao Geoghegan-Hart, Giro d'Italia champion) is now our Red Jersey and Vuelta Espana leader. Roglic, having a bad day, on a horrible day, losing time to both them and Dan Martin. He sits fourth, with Martin a single notch higher up.

Even by the standards of the Vuelta Espana 2020 this was a chaotic stage made doubly so by the weather and our complete inability to pick out one cyclist from another. Tomorrow's rest day comes at a welcome moment. It gives the riders half a chance of getting warm and dry in time for Stage 7 on Tuesday.

Carthy, in that understated way that he has, just looked a bit nonplussed. As if the weather conditions hadn't really occurred to him. Wondering what all the fuss was about.

Standings after Stage 6

Red Jersey: Richard Carapaz

2nd Hugh Carthy (+18 seconds)

3rd Dan Martin (+20 seconds)

Green (sprint/points): Primoz Roglic

Polka Dots (mountains): Tim Wellens

Stages 7-9: From the Basque Country, into Wide-Open Space

7: Michael Woods and the breakaway-deluxe

"Shake hands with him and you'd better count your fingers afterwards," said Eurosport's Carlton Kirby of Spaniard Omar Fraile (Astana). "Gentleman off the bike, absolute VILLAIN on it!"

But villainy, in the end, was beaten by the big heart of Canadian climber Michael Woods (EF Pro Cycling); because good guys, contrary to received wisdom, do win. But how on earth did Woods and Fraile find themselves duking it out at the finish in Villanueva de Valdegovia, across the Basque border and into Burgos, I hear you ask?

Well. You'll be familiar with the standard composition of a first week Vuelta Espana breakaway: a couple of plucky Spaniards from BH-Burgos or Caja Rural; a wily veteran; maybe a young buck on the up or an unheralded Scandinavian with a rumoured fast finish. Today was different. This was, as breakaways go, a supergroup. A breakaway-deluxe. A luxury escape-away. Alejandro Valverde, Sepp Kuss, George Bennett (Team Jumbo-Visma), Rui Costa (UAE Team Emirates), Guillaume Martin,

Davide Formolo (UAE Team Emirates), Woods and Fraile, of course, and more. Names. Players. The chasing peloton slightly edgy at the thought of a General Classification contender turned plucky breakaway chancer making big time gains.

The group, and the circumstances, made for a super-fast day. Rugged, windy, and autumnal. With ten kilometres to go and with the last of the climbs ticked off we had five of our A-listers clear. Valverde and Fraile; stone-cold killers. Guillaume Martin and Mick Woods; thoroughly lovely chaps, climbers who must attack long to win. And Nans Peters (AG2R La Mondiale); the big bruising Frenchman, hanging on a bit, if we're honest.

Come the business end Fraile was cold and decisive in his moves. Following mini-attacks, letting others go, calculating like an assassin on a bicycle. The street-smart wise-ass to the goofy chancers around him. Valverde, of course, possesses that same, ice cold heart, but carries it around these days on middle-aged legs. The ageing Movistar man surely two years out of date.

And then, from a kilometre out, Woods launched himself. Long, and straight. Fraile blinked inopportunely and looked up to see the Pink of EF Pro Cycling twenty metres clear. Kicking himself, he whipped out his sniper's rifle, took aim, and...missed!

He chased and lost, is what I'm saying.

Woods too far gone and helped by a mild climb to the finish line. The Canadian former runner outsmarting the fast-finishing Spaniard. There'll be (virtual, Covid-safe) handshakes all-round tonight, but next time they meet on the bike Woods better watch his back. And count his fingers, of course.

8: faster, harder, quicker

You have to hand it to those charge of the Vuelta; they know exactly what they're doing. They know that in the sixty days since the start of the Tour de France we have seen, as of this morning, forty-nine days of Grand Tour bike racing. Across France, Italy, and now Spain. Even those of us whose lives revolve around the sport are flagging a little.

And so, on Stage 8, it seemed reasonable we might be tempted to tune in just for the last fifteen kilometres or so. Just to keep in touch and get a feel for it. We would see fifteen minutes of Team Movistar lining up a reduced fifty-strong peloton for a ragged old climb up Alto de Moncalvillo. Eight kilometres in length, with ramps of twelve percent, then fifteen, and up to eighteen. The kind of climb that you almost feel bad for watching, as the riders suffer like skinny dogs for your watching pleasure.

You soon get over these feelings of sympathy and find yourself screaming at the telly. Suggesting your favourite riders should: "Pedal faster," "try harder," and "be quicker!" That sort of thing.

Were you, like me, shouting at Hugh Carthy? Thought so. He, with five kilometres remaining, took all three pieces of your advice and set his man Mike Woods to work in his service. Then, at the opportune moment, he struck out for glory. "That's it Hugh," we confirmed, "faster, harder, and if at all possible quicker."

He shouldn't have listened.

He'd gone too early.

From that point the stage was carnage. Tense, exciting, carnage. Carapaz and Roglic took turns to take wild swings at each other. Attack, and counter attack. Carthy and nodding dog Dan Martin close behind. Alexandr Vlasov the interloper in yet one more mighty General Classification contest. At the finish, last man standing was Roglic. Grimacing with the pain of it all. Crossing the line to win and remembering – a touch too late – to raise his arms and celebrate. Maybe all this racing has numbed his excitement too. Or maybe that's just what an almighty battle with Richard Carapaz can do to a man.

Whatever. We have a top four of Carapaz, Roglic, Martin and Carthy, separated by less than a minute, and with another thirteen stages of Grand Tour bike racing in this exhausting, compressed season. The Vuelta, no doubt, with further tricks up its sleeve.

9: largely quiet, and then suddenly very loud

The autonomous community of Castile and Leon, as we noted back on Stage 3, is big, and empty. People, for some reason, don't live here. As the peloton rolled gently through agricultural stripes of farmland and past mild geological features, we detected all the signs of a day off.

A pair of unheralded Spaniards headed up the road to fulfil the required roll of 'break.' Reeled-in with twenty kilometres to go, even then the peloton continued a stately progress. No sniping attacks. Spread wide, defensively across the road, this was to be a whole lot of not very much followed by five kilometres of Deceuninck-Quickstep versus Bora-Hansgrohe, for their sprinters Sam Bennett and Pascal Ackermann.

Look, what do you want me to say?

I would love to describe a swooping acceleration into an atmospheric, beautifully perched Spanish town, but I can't. Apologies to the people of these parts, who I'm sure are very lovely. But Aguilar de Campoo had the look of a functional, lightly industrial kind of place. If there was charm afoot it was well hidden. Big, wide main roads. A near deserted out of town street scene lined with manufacture and brutal practicality. A finish line, nowhere, populated by no-one (and it's Covid, of course, so I get the lack of people, but still...).

Into the finish, we hadn't seen Sam Bennett for a good while, which meant only one thing. He was hidden, tucked away in consummate control, and would appear from behind a lead-out man with two-hundred metres to go to sweep clear and win. The brutal predictability of a highly confident sprinter.

He was hidden. He appeared. He won.

Or so we thought. The race commissaires had a good old look at video replay and relegated our celebrated Irish sprinter for over-aggression in the face of mild opposition. Emils Liepins, Trek-Segafredo's Latvian sprinter, on the receiving end. And even then, in the spirit of a lethargic day, tempers seemed largely un-frayed.

Pascal Ackermann, of Bora, promoted to Stage winner, sympathised with Bennett. The Quickstep man himself was seen debating, firmly but fairly, with the officials who'd sent him packing. A general sense of "look, this 'aint ideal, but we've all had enough of mass finish-line sprint-finish pile-ups haven't we..." and a quiet acceptance of the decision.

It was left to Patrick Lefevere, Bennett's team boss – the man with the words "outspoken, irascible Belgian" in the 'occupation' column on his passport - to inject a dose of aggression into proceedings. Lefevere rarely holds back when things don't go the way of his team, and he quickly called "bullshit!" He was soon ranting on Twitter, asking the Trek team boss, less than classily, how many sprints Liepins has won, and spewing sarcasm and bile into an already saturated Twitter-sphere.

Sure, it was day very much in need of a dose of passion, but I'm not sure that's any way for a sixty-five-year-old bloke to behave.

Standings after Stage 9

Red Jersey: Richard Carapaz

2nd Primoz Roglic (+13 seconds)

3rd Dan Martin (+28 seconds)

Green (sprint/points): Primoz Roglic

Polka Dots (mountains): Guillaume Martin

Stages 10-12: North, to the Angliru

10: Primoz Roglic is The Man

We could do with some kind of wacky moustache notification system. Surely the big tech companies can solve this for us. Because how else are the fans supposed to identify our favourite cyclists following the growth of a daft 'tache? Sure, you might say I should have spotted Remi Cavagna's (Deceuninck-Quickstep) facial growth before today, but I didn't. And so, when he galloped away off the front of the race with ten kilometres to go, I was clueless.

"Some Quickstep lad," I thought, "but who is that strong, and that recklessly bold, but also in possession of such hastily thrown together facial hair?" I fed it through the part of my brain responsible for ID'ing cyclists (a part which, after a full-on few weeks of this time-crunched season, is pretty much running on fumes anyway), and came up blank.

Cavagna, apparently. Huh!? Apple, Google, Huawei...if you're listening, we need tiny top lip sensors please, which will notify us of growth and provide a digital photofit rendering of the offending cyclist to allow accurate ID. I know you're busy with AI and machine learning and all that, but this is important.

Away from Cavagna's face, I should report, there was also bike race on the go. And it was a tough one. Your first glance of today's route profile may had led you to expect a standard issue sprint stage but this, in Cantabria, is the Atlantic coast. Maybe you've walked (or even ridden) such terrain? If so, you'll know it is constantly either up, or down, and your knees will tell you all about it in the evening. A tough ol' day on the push iron.

Still, some sprinters were being talked about for the win. The hard final kilometre might just be race-able for the likes of Sam Bennett and Pascal Ackermann. Alas, Bennett went out the back with over thirty kilometres to go. Fighting agonisingly, sweating profusely, and looking frankly unwell, this was not his day. We wait to see whether this was a single bad day, one pint of Guinness too many, or something more terminal for the rest of the race.

Ackermann, meanwhile, was nowhere to be seen at the finish in the town of Suances. Guillaume Martin and Richard Carapaz were making the moves – climbers, and General Classification men – rather than sprinters. Cavagna's hairy escape long since shut down. And then Primoz Roglic appeared; the reigning Vuelta champion looking thoroughly regal, mightily strong, and barely out of breath.

For a man who had his heart well and truly broken by Tadej Pogacar at the Tour de France this year he looks firmly in possession of both his mojo and the fabled 'good legs'. His win, and small-time gain, drew him level overall with Carapaz and into the Red Jersey based on superior stage finish positions. Right now, the only thing that could spoil the dominant sight of the Slovenian would be a confusing charity moustache a la Cavagna. And as we know, the tech giants are on that for us.

For the weekend, and Stages 11 and 12, we have two days of brutal mountains which culminate with the appalling slopes of the Alto de l'Angliru. Right now, Roglic looks like 'The Man'. Forty-eight hours from now we will know for sure.

Race Radio

Guillaume Martin is Visible

Since around 2016 Guillaume Martin has been a fixture on the pro cycling circuit. Riding for Wanty-Groupe Gobert, and now Cofidis, he's hovered around on the radar of your average pro cycling fan. In name, at least, if not as one who might be recognised in civilian society. Not famous, but familiar.

"Ah yes," we might affect, in lieu of any actually insight, "Guillaume Martin...solid rider, good climber, decent pro."

Most of us knew little about the man beyond that Gallic name cropping up in commentary, but we enjoyed feigning recognition of the esoteric philosophy-student-cum-writer-cum-bike-racer: Martin is the author of 'Socrate en velo,' a work of fiction based around a bike race featuring teams of philosophers; Socrates, Descartes, Nietzsche, and the like. This Parisian pro cyclist is part-time public intellectual. Very French. Insert your own jokes here about Gauloise cigarettes and boozy afternoons in Les Deuz Magots.

For a few years, when not musing on the finer points of being and nothingness, Martin has been greedily gathering top ten finishes at middle ranking bike races, never quite breaking the big time, but now, riding for Cofidis, finds himself (almost) front and (nearly) centre.

He announced himself pre-Tour de France with third overall at the Criterium du Dauphine. Impressive. At the Tour itself he had a good old stab at winning Stage 4 and sat firmly in the top three overall before losing time on Stage 13. He was there, day after day, on our TV screens, an ephemeral will'o-the-wisp made flesh before our eyes. His ultimate eleventh placed finish marks him out as an official Tour de France General Classification contender. And not too many cyclists have that little tagline in their locker.

And here, deep into the Vuelta, he's at it again. In the thick of the action. Animating the race. Visible. He's been up the road and on the attack and finds himself as a commanding wearer of the Polka Dot jersey. Leaving stage wins to the likes of Roglic, Carthy and Carapaz, but diligently mopping up points on just about every preceding climb. Clinical.

No longer will we feign knowledge and patronise his abilities.

"Ah yes," we'll say, "Guillaume Martin...audacious and attacking, decent climber and a good tactician. Knows his way around a Grand Tour. Dark, swarthy, French-looking chap...you can't miss him."

11: fun on the Farrapona

Too tough to be fun. For both riders and viewers. Three first category climbs led us to a summit finish on the fourth; the Alto de Farrapona, a great Asturian brute of a slope. This was not a day for whimsical attacks up the road. This was a grinding war of two-wheeled attrition, and no rider with Red Jersey ambitions would risk blowing up today.

The mighty Jumbo-Visma juggernaut was in full flow. With five kilometres to go Primoz Roglic was surrounded by three of his teammates while Richard Carapaz, of Ineos, was alone. The general idea was to sit on the wheels and fight like hell in the final, steep kilometres of the stage to avoid a time loss. That's not to say we didn't have some enjoyment.

Marc Soler, for example, I find to be a workable form of entertainment in and of himself. There's something about him. That gormless, mouth-agape; the raggedy breathe-strip across his nose; those rounded, undeveloped shoulders, suggesting a life devoted to literally nothing other than riding a bicycle; and the gazelle like pedal stroke, his body and bike following the whimsy of those long legs.

With five kilometres to go he leapt clear from the breakaway group of five and was quickly joined by French up-and-comer David

Gaudu (Groupama-FDJ). Soler was simultaneously on the cusp of a second stage win of this race and a nice little catapult up the leader board, and about to be ripped to shreds by the cold calculation of Gaudu.

The Frenchman had the look of a chess Grandmaster setting a trap. Soler had wandered, queen first, into a hive of knights and rooks, and no amount of defensive pawn work would save him.

That is not to diminish a superb effort from the loveable Soler. He had made the break, driven the break, and then instigated the winning move. Credit where it's due. And for Gaudu, stepping from the shadow of his superstar team-leader Thibaut Pinot, it was a win of absolute class. Strong, decisive, and maybe the kind of ride to give the bosses at Groupama FDJ a little something to think about, Pinot-wise? As in, 'the king is dead, long live the king?'

We shall see. Tomorrow, Stage 12, is another brute. The finale will see them hit the twelve kilometre long Alto d'Angliru. It's final six kilometres average thirteen percent in gradient. There are ramps up to twenty-four percent; slopes so steep that simply following the wheels in front will not be available as a tactic. It will be every man for himself.

Some riders will lose minutes, hours, maybe even days. Others will scrap and scramble up the leader-board. Availability of teammates will be a moot point. To kill yourself in a breakaway today with that on the menu tomorrow was bold indeed. Possibly stupid. Suicidal, even?

Tomorrow, stuff will happen. It might not be pretty. But as long as you like your entertainment sprinkled with a little masochism, you'll be happy.

Waiting for Gaudu

Where is Thibaut Pinot, you might be wondering? Our favourite French contender, so good when he's good, seemingly crushed by the pressure of it all when things go bad, had this Vuelta pegged as a form of redemption for 2020. After a Stage 1 crash, a back injury, and an out-of-contention solo lap around France at the Tour, this race was to be a reset. Riding in support of his able lieutenant David Gaudu he would salvage pride and find some fun on the roads of Spain.

Alas, poor Thibaut, we knew him well. Still troubled by back pain he lost twenty-five minutes on the opening two stages and abandoned. And we wonder, are we seeing Pinot's terminal decline? Are the days of the Groupama FDJ team being built around his (let's not forget, considerable) talents numbered?

At the Giro, we saw Arnaud Demare stake a huge claim that this team should be sprint focussed, should revolve around him, and to hell with ambitions of overall Grand Tour victory. And here, with his Stage 11 victory, Pinot's twenty-four-year-old mountain helper David Gaudu has provided another jab in the ribs to team bosses who may have the next big French thing on their hands.

Fifth overall at the Tour de Romandie and sixth at Liege Bastogne Liege last year. Forth at the UAE tour earlier in 2020. A former winner (in 2016) of the Tour de l'Avenir – the Tour of the Future, a prestigious event designed to root out young, potential Grand Tour contenders. The boy has pedigree.

It would be a shame if we've had the best of Pinot. He's a rider of great humanity and prodigious talent. Go and YouTube his wins at Il Lombardia in 2018, or atop the Tourmalet at the 2019 Tour de France. Spin tingling stuff. But the signs point to a punch-drunk boxer unable to drag himself from the canvas one more time. We shall see.

David Gaudu waits patiently in the wings.

12: Hugh Carthy tames the Angliru

Everything you've heard about the Angliru is true; it's a terrible climb. In a world of exaggeration and hyperbole it is genuinely epic, brutal, and potentially life shortening. You could easily tackle the lower slopes in perfect health only to find you've acquired a heart condition by the summit. That kind of climb. There is little to compare it to.

Just consider the stats for a moment: it's twelve kilometres in length and the final six average thirteen percent in gradient. For a couple of kilometres, it doesn't drop below seventeen, and contains ramps up to almost twenty-four percent. Pro riders, when cornered and asked for an opinion, generally lapse into the thousand-year stare of man who's seen things he wishes he could unsee before running off for a little cry.

You get the idea?

Today, on Stage 12, it was our big finish. Well in advance of the final slopes we were down to our top six General Classification contenders (and Roglic's teammate Sepp Kuss, of course). From the side-on TV view the torture was apparent; each rider locked in his own world, grinding to a halt between every pedal stroke, any pretence at momentum long since cast aside by those damn inconvenient laws of physics.

The final two or three kilometres were about finding a coping pace - a sustainable level of effort - and riding at that. Anything more would be suicide. Unless your name is Hugh Carthy, who thought to himself: "yeah, this seems ok...might throw in a little attack here lads!" And off he went. In slow motion. Eeking out the metres between himself and Richard Carapaz and Enric Mas, who in turn were few bike lengths clear of Dan Martin, Aleksandr Vlasov, and the battling Roglic (and the trusty Kuss, of course).

The moment when Carthy rounded a torturous right hander near the summit, face overwhelmed by grimace, the glory of Asturias opening up behind him in dramatic backdrop, might be my single favourite moment of Grand Tour racing this season. The claustrophobic wall of Asphalt giving way to the wider world; a world where things other than pain and suffering exist, and we knew he'd nearly won. It was beautiful.

And I'm biased, of course, because Carthy is a Lancashire lad (like me) and I know tons of cyclists who look like him, speak like him, and would give an agreed percentage of their salary to be able to ride a bike like him. Wonderful stuff!

Carthy now lies third overall in this Vuelta Espana. To leap two further places might be a task too far, but I guess when you've won on the Angliru it probably feels like anything's possible. Alternatively, you might decide you never want to go anywhere near a bicycle (or a mountain) ever again. Both of these are acceptable responses.

Standings after Stage 12

Red jersey: Richard Carapaz

2nd Primoz Roglic (+10 seconds)

3rd Hugh Carthy (+32 seconds)

Green (sprint/points): Primoz Roglic

Polka Dots (mountains): Guillaume Martin

Stages 13-15: Galicia

13: the tremble-o-meter

For a short while today we obsessed over how quickly each rider could dismount one bike, mount another, clip in, and ride away with a hefty shove from track-suited team-lackey. In a niche area of the sport (time-trialling) the race organisers gave us an extra layer of niche.

Because today's TT route, from Muros to Mirador de Ezaro, in the Galician north-west corner of Spain, comprised 31.9 pan flat kilometres followed by 1.8 super steep ones. It was a little beauty of a course.

The bike change for the final climb was a no-brainer − of course there was advantage to be had from swapping to a standard road bike − and Eurosport's Carlton Kirby was on the lookout for trembly legs. Legs that would indicate excessive tiredness. I half expected a tremble-o-meter to appear, bottom left, on screen.

The last time we watched Primoz Roglic time-trial uphill you may remember his entire world fell apart. It was Stage 20 of the Tour de France and his child-like countryman, Tadej Pogacar, handed him his rear-end on a plate. If we were to get a repeat performance today then Richard Carapaz and Hugh Carthy would be on hand to rub it in.

Carapaz, no time-trial expert, an ace on the climbs, went well. Seventh overall on the day. Carthy, long of leg and rictus faced, nailed fourth. He was flying. But Roglic, in the stock-still aero-tuck of a man with access to a wind-tunnel and a lot of time on his hands, was imperious. Fast on the flat, quick on the climb, he blitzed the course to win the stage and seize the leader's Red Jersey. He was even spotted grinning at the summit. Which, for Roglic, is a niche area of behaviour; the expressing of visible emotion not being within his usual bag o' tricks.

With that, we have five stages to go. Roglic leads by thirty-nine seconds from Carapaz and a further eight from Carthy. Remarkably, Roglic has now won four of the thirteen stages in this race, which is quite the strike rate. With only one genuine mountainous stage left (but also three typically tough hilly Vuelta days) he is the favourite. No doubt.

But you might have noticed it's been a funny old year. I, for one, formally retired from the predictions industry way back at the Tour de France. Let's just wait and see, eh?

14: Well, Well, Wellens

Yes...predicting bike races is a fool's game. Lots of variables, see. Form, tiredness, and fundamental talent being but three. Factor in everything else - terrain, sleep quality, wind direction, star sign, favourite colour – and it becomes a guessing game. And then sometimes, all those hours you spend watching bike racing fall into place. The details, perceptible and imperceptible, gather together like pixels to complete the image of the winner-to be. As with Tim Wellens today.

With twenty kilometres to go the peloton had clocked off. Spread wide across the wide, the internationally recognised cycling symbol for 'sod it chaps, let the breakaway have it today,' The winner would come from our six-man escape. The General Classification contenders would hover, three minutes in arrears, and call a truce.

The stage was classic Vuelta. Up and down across Galicia, all day, nothing resembling a mountain and yet three-thousand metres and more of vertical ascent. Sean Kelly, Eurosport hype-man and Hardest Man In The World, called it a real leg breaker. He is not a man to over-describe a bike ride. If Kelly says it's hard then trust me...it's hard.

As our six headed towards the finish town of Ourense they quietly became three, and that offered our first Wellens-related clue. Zdenek Stybar (Deceuninck-Quickstep) and Marc Soler clipped sneakily clear and the Belgian was the one to react. He launched off down the road, TT'ing across to the pair alone and latching on. He made this move not in a panicked 'shit, hang on...wait for me' kind of way. This was a calculated effort in response to a dangerous attack. No drama.

I should mention, at this point, that this was no ordinary breakaway. It featured Wellens, Marc Soler, Zdenek Stybar, Michael Woods, Dylan van Baarle (Ineos Grenadiers), and Thyman Arensman. Big hitters.

To the base of our steep finale – a tough finishing ramp, Wellens-esque in length and placement – three suddenly became six again. Cat and mouse being a key component of any good bike race. Still Wellens was the pick. There was something serene about his movements among this small (yet stellar) group. The other five, by now, had perhaps noticed that particularly winning-y aura around him. What we all saw, I think, was the fabled 'good legs' and experienced brain on a route that might have been accurately described in the road book as: 'Stage 14: a celebration of Tim Wellens.'

With five-hundred metres to go he moved, like a lion, from sixth place to first. And then waited. An apex predator surrounded by gazelles (but gazelles on bikes...just go with me on this). The very moment one of them twitched (Marc Soler, as it happens, afraid he would end up as lunch), Wellens stomped on the power and assumed control. Michael Woods gave chase, and got close, whilst also never really being in contention.

Wellens winning, as we knew he would, with entertaining predictability.

15: the hardest bastard in Spain

I see what the Vuelta bosses are doing in this final week. Rather than a succession of vertiginous mountain adventures they've gone for something more attritional. A succession of rugged, aggressively lumpy stages will give way, on Saturday, to a high-altitude summit finish on the Alto de la Covatilla. That stage, the seventeenth and penultimate, will decide the winner of the Vuelta Espana. Right now, the riders are being tenderised like a cheap cut of meat in preparation for the pot. Today, Stage

15, we had additional ingredients: a relentless headwind, plenty of rain, fog, and a proper chill in the air. A hard, hard bastard of a day.

Riders were unidentifiable in a leg warmers and jackets, most of them just happy to get their head down and pedal. A small group of overall contenders stayed alert on time-loss avoidance duties. And a select group of total nutters were well up for it and fancied a stage win. Imagine peeling back the hotel curtains on a day like today and rubbing your hands at the sight: "oh yes...can't wait to race the ol' bikes today chaps, and I fancy a win!"

Different breed.

In the end Stage 15 was, oddly, a sprint stage. Kind of. But not like the one in your mind's eye. This was not some pan-flat approach to a luxurious and muscular boulevard finish. This was a ragged, last man standing affair.

Over the final climb and down the other side Italian hard man Mattia Cattaneo (Deceuninck-Quickstep) was clear, the last of the day's break, and looking like our winner. A lead of a minute and a half and with a largely downhill fifteen kilometres to the finish. But the infernal headwind saw it differently. His form began to fray at the edges. The biggest win of this thirty-year old pro's career unravelled before us, cruelly, on this tough, grim November day. He'd grafted like a Welsh miner for nothing.

Into the finish town of Puebla de Sanabria, near the northern Portuguese border, came an already thin peloton. Hand wringing and hunkered down, a lot of cold, tired cyclists were already mentally checking into the post stage hotel. Just a few tough guy sprinters really wanted it.

On a greasy, technical run-in, Teams UAE and Bora-Hansgrohe unleashed a kind of tentative aggression. Their men Jasper Phillipsen and Pascal Ackermann gently bumped and politely barged each, being sure not to end up sprawled on wet Tarmac, before Phillipsen launched from a mile out (ok, maybe 250 metres). With a bullish burst of brute force, he took the biggest win of his young career.

And, of course, the coveted title of 'Hardest Bastard in Spain.'

Standings after Stage 15

Red Jersey: Primoz Roglic

2nd Richard Carapaz (+39 seconds)

3rd Hugh Carthy (+47 seconds)

Green (sprint/points): Primoz Roglic

Polka Dots (mountains): Guillaume Martin

Roglic Has Got History

Had you come to this Vuelta Espana without the benefit of context, and with a reckless urge to visit your favourite bookmaker and stick the mortgage on a rake-thin pro athlete for kicks, you'd pick Primoz Roglic. No question. He looks strong of body, iron of will, and is surrounded by a powerful phalanx of highly paid lieutenants to shepherd him through.

Frankly, any rider who has the mighty, near superhuman Sepp Kuss as a willing teammate, is at a distinct advantage. Sure, Richard Carapaz (former Giro d'Italia winner) and Hugh Carthy (laconic, leggy, and hugely talented) are putting up a hell of a fight, but Roglic is the big favourite.

He also, lest we forget, has history.

Not only did he suffer utter collapse on Stage 20 of this year's Tour de France from a mighty winning position, he has previous in that regard. He faltered badly, as favourite, at the 2019 Giro. In between times, of course, he won the Vuelta Espana of 2019. He's a big, alpha male of a bike racer, but without the dominance of Froome in his pomp. He's not flaky, as such, but neither is he a sure thing.

I'd still advise you to wager your house on him winning, more for reasons of entertainment than common sense. My mortgage is staying firmly where I left it. I'm just saying the Richard Carapaz could also win. And this being 2020, year of WTF, I wouldn't totally rule out Hugh Carthy.

So...feelin' lucky?

Stages 16-18: Tired Legs for the Big Finish

16: Magnus Cort Neilsen is the least tired

Yesterday, a couple of sprinters – Philipsen and Ackerman – made it over the hills to contest a sprint. Today, Stage 16, the mountains were too much. A peloton shorn of riders hit the finish in Ciudad Rodrigo. A small, tired gaggle of the fastest remaining finishers would contest the finish. The General Classification contenders tucked in, politely watching on.

It's a little strange to spend so much of this final week without shots fired in the overall classification. For three relentless days now we've had tough riding, over terrain with nothing selective enough to tempt a Roglic, a Carapaz, or a Carthy to make a move. Yesterday the riders had reported desperately cold conditions. Stage 16 was similar to Stage 15 only with slightly bigger hills and significantly better weather; any suffering today, I'd suggest, was well within the realms of the profession. Painful, but wholly acceptable. Far beyond what most of us would accept during a day at work, but standard for a pro.

You start to see, at this point in a tough Grand Tour, who can recover and stay strong, and who is done. The rear of this peloton is now dotted daily with riders on the wane, just surviving. I won't name names out of respect. Up front, meanwhile, a whole other group. You can see in the pedal stroke of race-leader Primoz Roglic, for example, that the spring remains in his stroke. Propelling himself forward, momentum on tap. Tired – surely, he has to be – but still with a snap in his tendons.

Remi Cavagna, too, still looks energetic. When he dropped breakaway companion Rob Stannard in the final twenty kilometres to ride clear of the race today, his strength appeared bottomless. No tell-tale waggles or squaring up of pedal-stroke he looked like he might, just might, win the stage. Perhaps attempting to avenge the tragic death of teammate Cattaneo yesterday, from an identical position.

Figuratively speaking, that is. To be clear, no-one died.

The Frenchman (now sans facial hair...make your mind up Remi lad!) fought like a poked bear only to be swept up, and with a shake of the head (berating himself in the third person - you must try harder, Remi) was caught with two kilometres to go. From there, a random band of non-sprinters sprinted. Tiredness, at the finish, to the fore. Muscles aching, wooden legged, this was the finale of a group of tired cyclists unable to hide their tiredness any more.

Valverde had a look, Dion Smith (Mitchelton-Scott) was interested, only for Magnus Cort Neilsen, in this wonderful race for his team EF Pro Cycling, to swing right and claim his crown as the least tired of all the tired men. Career Vuelta Stage win number three for him, and the third of the race for his team.

And remember how I said the General Classification men were unconcerned with making a move? Roglic snuck through in second place for six bonus seconds and a small extension to his race lead. What a pro. Tomorrow is Stage 17, our penultimate stage in a circumstance-shortened Grand Tour. Perhaps other, less alert cyclists, are working on the usual twenty-one-stage schedule. Because from now, there is little opportunity to sneak a time gap. Bonus seconds are gold dust. And that, right there, from Roglic, was (potential) Vuelta-winning behaviour.

17: Roglic by a whisker

When the riders crossed the line at the summit of la Covatilla here on Stage 17, they dropped their guard of athletic impregnability and became human beings again. Tired, relieved, and close to completion of a tough, tough Vuelta. Game faces fell away to reveal the chinks of humanity. A quick chat between Primoz Roglic and Richard Carapaz, a smiling acknowledgement from race winner to nearly, so nearly, late snatcher of that crown, to say: 'well done pal, you had me shitting me'self there for a minute!'

I particularly enjoyed the gloriously low-key Hugh Carthy, as ever, catching his breath, mingling, happy to have left it all out on the road to secure third place in this hectic Vuelta Espana. Each interaction with every eager journalist delivered with the arch air of: 'I honestly have no idea why on earth you want to ask me questions, but you seem keen so I suppose I'll oblige.'

It was Carthy, of the main contenders, who'd initially lit this stage up. The slopes of the Covatilla, our summit finish, had been oppressive; cloaked in fog, thick with mizzle, a grim-faced grind at a pace from which the idea of attack seemed wishful. Carthy, on the limit though he was, clearly had no desire to ride the final three kilometres as a coronation of Roglic's race lead, and off he went. Immediately the clouds cleared, the sun shone through, and our collective mood lifted.

Following Carthy's lead others took their turn. Enric Mas had a little look. Roglic hovered, either about to crack or ride away, it was hard to say. And then, with two kilometres to go, second placed man Carapaz found a burst of acceleration and dug deep into his reserves of Ecuadorian energy. And we all recalled, as one, that Roglic, on occasion, has been known to fade. He slumped at the 2019 Giro from a position of strength. He blew up at the Tour against compatriot Pogacar. Would he falter? Surely not this time?

"Go Carapaz...Go Roglic!" I heard myself yell, loving the drama and jeopardy of the possible overhauling of Roglic's forty-odd second race lead, and unable to bear the dejection that might be about to be heaped on the Slovenian. "And GO HUGH, ALSO..." I continued, wanting more than anything to see Carthy deliver the kind of surprise not seen since an ambitious lad called Moses found himself faced by the Red Sea and with the boat rental place shut.

Miracles happen. But not quite today. Carapaz would half the deficit to Roglic to finish second. Carthy would beat Roglic to the line to clinch third. And Roglic would remain strong (just) and composed (only just) and, barring accident in Madrid, the winner of this Vuelta.

Up the road, meanwhile, Frenchman David Gaudu, a powerful remnant of a huge early breakaway, would win the stage in emphatic style. Win number two of his race. To mention Gaudu as a footnote seems harsh. His race has been a double-stage winning and eventual eighth place overall finishing triumph. He has politely, respectfully, and powerfully edged out from team leader Pinot's shadow, and perhaps taken his place as Grand Tour leader of that team.

But today, after a week of stalemate, was about the winner of the Vuelta Espana. Primoz Roglic, after seventeen stages, by twenty-four tiny, tightly-contested seconds.

18: Madrid

Laps around Madrid, back-slaps, photo-ops: you know the script. As the riders swallowed up the city streets, the late autumnal sunshine slanted across the Spanish capital and we reflected on Primoz Roglic retaining his Vuelta title.

The most predictable winner of the three Grand Tours of 2020 (the others being the stone-cold surprises of Tadej Pogacar and Tao Geoghegan-Hart) proving, in the language of early-noughties English football, he has 'bounceback-ability.' To see the broken, shattered version of Roglic after he'd had his bum smacked by young Pogacar back at the Tour was to wonder whether he might ever drag himself out of bed again, never mind win another bike race. On that occasion a life-changing achievement had slipped through his grasp like a luxury bar of soap in a shower. The world watching on as he fumbled around near the plughole, undignified, and unable to retrieve the situation.

And yet, from that shattering event he came back to perform well at the World Championships, win Liege-Bastogne-Liege – a prestigious monument of one-day classics cycling - and now the Vuelta. If anyone ever asks you to define character, talk them through the soap/shower metaphor and tell them about Roglic in 2020.

Richard Carapaz, the Ineos man, took second, on the day of teammate Chris Froome's final race with the team. Froome moves on to Israel Start-up Nation for 2021 and hopes, desperately, that the injuries suffered at his big crash of 2019 have not derailed hopes of Tour de France win number five.

Third overall was the mighty Hugh Carthy; gangly, northern, and totally comfortable in his role as slightly perplexed no-nonsense voice of reason. While others lose their tiny minds over his rise to prominence (like me, when he won on the Angliru for example...WHOOP!), he responds with a raise of the eyebrow and a quick exit for a cup of tea on the team bus. I hope he stays with the slightly random, rebellious EF Pro Cycling. I hope he remains social media free. Never change, Hugh lad.

As for today, the final stage, the sprinters did their thing on the wide Madrileno roads. Respect is due to these guys, who've dragged themselves across the hills and mountains of Spain for days on end now, for no reward other than the chance, a ticket in the raffle, to win the sprint in Madrid. Deceuninck-Quickstep, Bora-Hansgrohe, and Team Sunweb had a stern jawed arm-wrestle for a few kilometres before the two class sprinters in the race – Sam Bennett and Pascal Ackermann – went pedal for pedal for the win. A lunge, a bike throw, and Ackermann took it by six inches.

Vuelta Espana Final Standings

Red Jersey: Primoz Roglic

2nd Richard Carapaz (+24 seconds)

3rd Hugh Carthy (+1 minute 15 seconds)

Green (sprint/points): Primoz Roglic

Polka dots (mountains): Guillaume Martin

It began, way back in the Basque country, as a knife fight. Our General Classification contenders, abandoning any thoughts of caution and strategy, chopped and sliced at each other without regard for self-preservation. The likes of Roglic, Carapaz, Carthy and Martin competed for stage wins and prestige while Marc Soler and Tim Wellens delivered punchy little cameos for no other reason than our entertainment. It was joyous, unbounded, and frankly a little exhausting.

Into week two things calmed down. Mountains were scaled. David Gaudu won on the Alto de la Farrrapona and Hugh Carthy delivered a total masterpiece on the fearsome Alto d'Angliru; a climb so storied and mythical, it was atmospheric even without a crowd – Covid restrictions, as they were for most of this race, being rigorously enforced. Had Carthy done that on a road eight deep with fans we can only imagine the excitement.

And then, a curious third week. Relentlessly rugged with hills, thousands of metres of ascent each day, but barely a selective climb to be found. The hardest terrain in the world delivered precisely nothing to separate Roglic, Carapaz and Carthy on the road. The denouement, on the penultimate stage climb to the Alto de la Covatilla, with riders beaten up and drained of spark, was too little after too much. Carapaz tried to win, but Roglic was secure.

This race, with its odd rhythm, boiled down in hindsight to Primoz Roglic's diligent collection of bonus seconds en route. That, right there, was his winning margin. A slow burning slugfest and a victory for pragmatism. But the beauty of a Grand Tour is that even a slightly dull race can be rescued by the day-to-day skirmishes of a cast of characters. Tim Wellens doing Tim Wellens; Michael Woods mugging Omar Freile in **Villanueva de Valdegovia**; Hugh Carthy, like a length of pink spaghetti, bossing it on the Angliru.

In a season of shocks and surprises, a gritty Primoz Roglic victory is somewhat against the grain. We've come to expect more drama, more surprise, more NEW! But after his collapse at the Tour, on the brink of a career defining moment, it would take a cold heart indeed to deny him this.

Aaand breathe

Sixty Grand Tour stages in seventy-two days. Beginning in Nice, on August 29th, finishing in Madrid on the 8th November, and taking in all manner of towns, villages, hills, mountains, forests and flatlands in-between. To say this was a season like no other is stating the obvious. To use the word unprecedented is a little lazy. This rollercoaster of racing led us through all the usual emotions and then a few extra, lesser used ones: trepidation, germaphobia, epidemiological uncertainty...is that an emotion?

The entire historical Tour de France roll of honour contains eleven blanks. On account of the world being at war, this great race failed to take place twice between 1903 and 2019. As excuses not to ride your bike go, it's solid. Had you asked many wise observers in April, even May 2020, they might have predicted rounding the blanks up to an even dozen. Because this was the year that the virus took hold in Europe. Things of permanence and certainty fell one-by-one. Travel ceased; shops and schools closed; bars and restaurants pulled up the shutters; jobs ceased, with millions sent home on a Government pay-check.

For a good three months to simply leave one's own house took a permit (in some countries) or at least a damn good excuse (in many others). By the time 'lockdown' was established as a concept, the idea of cancelling the Tour de France (along with the Giro d'Italia, Vuelta Espana, and most other sporting events) had morphed from 'unthinkable' to 'unavoidable'. We discovered that the state, and its public health apparatus, carries an awful lot more clout than the governing body of a sport.

And then Europe slowly opened up. A late-August Tour was tentatively announced, to be followed by an October Giro that would overlap onto a Vuelta slated to finish in November. It was a plan, we agreed, but we wondered how far in (if at all) we would get before the combined health services of the continent would force an intervention.

Each Grand Tour, in its own way, wobbled at times: under the tension of rest-day Covid tests, the growing concern of public opinion, and the occasional outburst from riders and team staff. The wisdom of a travelling circus criss-crossing the continent was questioned. We cringed occasionally as fans got too close. Many removed their masks to better bellow at their sporting heroes, each mountain stage a potential super-spreader.

But slowly, as Tour became Giro morphed into Vuelta, a sense of calm normality seeped through. The idea of a one-hundred-and-eighty-strong peloton existing as a Covid-secure bubble still felt fanciful, but positive tests and exclamations of public doubt came in a trickle rather than a blizzard. With the Tour and Giro having reached Paris and Milan intact, much of the Vuelta took place amid an atmosphere of inevitable completion. The question of whether the race would reach Madrid ceased to be asked.

For those of us with no other obligation than to watch the action on the telly the pro cycling season served as a welcome window into what, for most of us in 2020, has been a small, shrinking world. The simple fact of a bike race rolling by in the corner of our living room offered a little snatch of escapism. A visual confirmation that it's all still out there. That towns and villages, from Brindisi to Salamanca via Gap, go about their business, navigating this anxiety-inducing and invisible threat, and will still be there – to visit, pass by, and race bikes through – on the other side.

Pre-season, we might have predicted a Primoz Roglic win at the Vuelta Espana, but we would never have imagined the total, utter collapse, at the Tour de France to his young countryman Tadej Pogacar. Stage 20, to La Planche des Belles Filles, was a stage for the ages. In between came the Giro d'Italia, with late twists and drama, that delivered Tao Geoghegan-Hart, through the streets of Milan, to win. File that one under 'never-saw-that-coming', sub-section 'couldn't-happen-to-a-nicer-chap.'

We, collectively, will remember 2020 as a mad, tragic year. The year the pandemic took hold. We should also, with a healthy dose of perspective, recall a fantastic year of Grand Tour bike racing. It didn't always feel like a good idea, but repeatedly caused us to jump from our seat and holler with joy. And some of us needed that.